BASIC PIANO
for the College Student

BASIC PIANO
for the College Student
Fourth Edition

Alex Zimmerman
University of Missouri

Russell Hayton
Montclair State College

Dorothy Priesing
Montclair State College

wcb

Wm. C. Brown Company Publishers
Dubuque, Iowa

MUSIC SERIES

Consulting Editor

Frederick Westphal
California State University, Sacramento

Contents

Introduction

Purpose of the Book

Basic Piano for the College Student is intended to improve the proficiency of the music student whose major is not piano and who is preparing to be a school music teacher.

Music school administrators indicate that most music students coming out of colleges and universities are noticeably deficient in the area of keyboard flexibility. Many music educators note the lack of keyboard efficiency as a real roadblock to competency and security in any area of music teaching.

Some three hundred and twelve music educators working as choral, band, orchestra, elementary and college teachers and specialists testified to the importance of keyboard skills in their positions.[1]

The respondents in the study also indicated the particular skills which they found most important for their success on the job. These skills were definitely those which are commonly called functional; for example, playing a simple accompaniment to a folk song in an elementary school songbook, sight-reading, transposing, playing an octavo score, playing a condensed band or orchestra score, and playing assembly songs by ear.

This exemplifies the need for curriculum changes in the approach to piano for the music education major. Less emphasis should be placed on playing scales and memorizing recital pieces and more emphasis should be given drill and intellectual competency in the functional skills. The ability to play Bach inventions, Beethoven sonatas, and to memorize repertoire does not assure the capacity for harmonizing melodies, improvising, playing scores and reading at sight.

This is not to deny the need for a certain degree of piano technical skill, but these skills can be acquired by types of standard piano literature which serves the dual purpose of strengthening technique and forming a part of the classroom repertoire of the student who ventures into the teaching field.

The keyboard harmony section of the book makes it a suitable supplementary text for music theory and keyboard harmony classes. In fact, the book could be used as part of a core curriculum text in which basic piano, keyboard harmony, analysis and all aspects of theory are presented in a meaningful way for the improvement of musicianship. It goes without saying, of course, that the book would be helpful to any study or person desirous of improving his functional piano skill.

In many colleges students who are not music majors are permitted to enter piano classes without the competencies in music fundamentals which music majors have. Consequently, a section on music fundamentals is included.

This volume, then, is designed to help strengthen the music student in the specific piano skills which will improve his musicianship and make him a better teacher.

---

[1]Gillian Buchanan, "Skills in Piano Performance in the Preparation of Music Educators," *Journal of Research in Music Education* 12:134–138, Summer, 1964.

How the Book Is Organized

This volume is organized into sections designed to improve certain proficiencies, techniques, keyboard harmony, sight-reading, and the like. This makes for great flexibility in the use of the book and enables the teacher to prescribe corrections for certain deficiencies in the student. The teacher, therefore, will assign work in various parts of the book as needed.

One outstanding feature of the book is found in the reading section, where the pieces are designed to be played completely by the more apt while other students may play only a single part. This makes the pieces duos, trios, or quartets. In addition, there is an ensemble section that makes it possible for the more competent student to remain an interested member of the class, while the less competent strive for improvement.

A unique feature of the book is the introduction of the modes for technical facility and in some simple modal compositions. These also serve as a first approach to modal analysis. Also included are some contemporary titles in addition to the standard keyboard literature.

Care has been taken to include materials which may be useful to the student when he takes over in the classroom.

How to Use the Book

While the volume has been planned and used by the authors as a class piano approach, the merit of the book for utilization by those who approach the problem on a one-to-one basis is quite obvious.

The class approach, however, has many values in its favor. One of these is the "pacing" that students set up in friendly rivalry and can serve as a motivating force. In this connection the authors have found the use of a tape recorder to be very effective. At certain designated class periods the students perform and are recorded individually in prescribed goals along the way to proficiency. This is most effective when the recording is made by each individual in front of the class, thus encouraging careful practice and preparation so as to perform well in the presence of peers.

Class piano means playing the piano in ensemble. Good sight-reading is based on the ever, on-flowing beat, and while playing in a group time does not allow halting at specific problem points. With repetition the halting spots are less formidable; and playing together has helped all students to more alert habits. Furthermore, constant playing during the class period provides many minutes of good practice for college music students who are already overharassed by termpapers, performances and so on. The group playing can be varied on occasion by having each student play a phrase or period of the piece on call by the teacher without losing the rhythm of the number being played. This makes for a very alert class.

All too often the teacher assigned to the piano class takes the traditional approach, and being unfamiliar with class piano procedure, turns in desperation and frustration to giving each student in the class a five-minute private lesson. Nothing is more sure to spell defeat for the objectives of functional piano skill.

The success of the piano student is almost directly proportionate to the number of minutes he is playing with his classmates during the class period. A minimum of talk by the teacher, a steady tempo which is reasonable for the stage of advancement of the student, an ear-consciousness on the part of the student to the playing of his fellows as well as to himself; all of these are essential to the advancement of the student.

A suggested list of weekly goals can help pace the student in his progress. Such a list is appended.

Transposition

Functional piano playing demands the ability to transpose. Transposition means playing the same material in other keys.

Good transposing skill depends on:

1. Observations before playing:
   a. New key signature.
   b. Meter signature.
   c. Tempo markings.
   d. Shape and direction of melodic lines.
   e. Shape and direction of chords and chord resolutions.
2. Setting a tempo suited to the stage of advancement: Set tempo slow enough to permit complete coordination between eye, brain, and fingers. "Halting" playing will not produce good transposition ability. Speed comes after coordination is established.
3. Keeping your eyes on the score.
4. Locating the keys by touch.
5. Reading horizontally, not vertically. Awareness of shape and direction of the original version is a must for good transposition. Under no condition should the student transpose each note as a separate item.

Fundamentals

The Great Staff

The location of note symbols on the staff indicates precise pitches. In piano music these pitches are shown on the *Great Staff*. This consists of a staff with a treble clef and a staff with a bass clef combined. The pitches used in piano literature are all written on the great staff or below or above it with ledger lines.

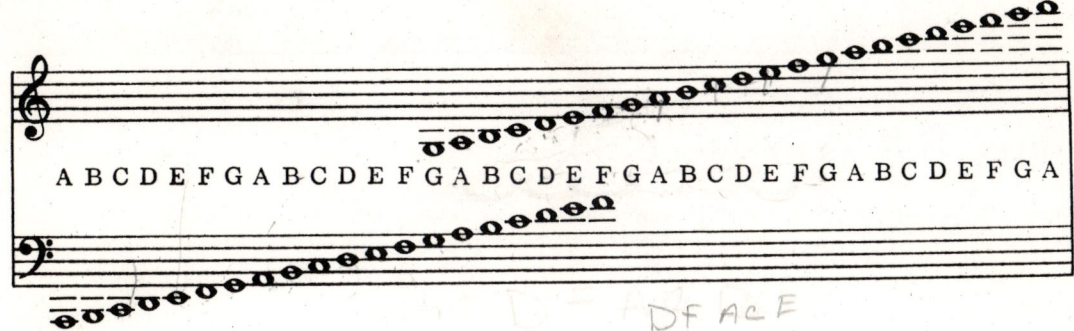

A B C D E F G A B C D E F G A B C D E F G A B C D E F G A B C D E F G A

The Keyboard

The basic letter names of the pitches are all on the white keys of the keyboard and the sharps and flats are all on the black keys. The black key is named from the white key immediately below raised a half-step by a sharp, or from the white key immediately above lowered a half-step by a flat.

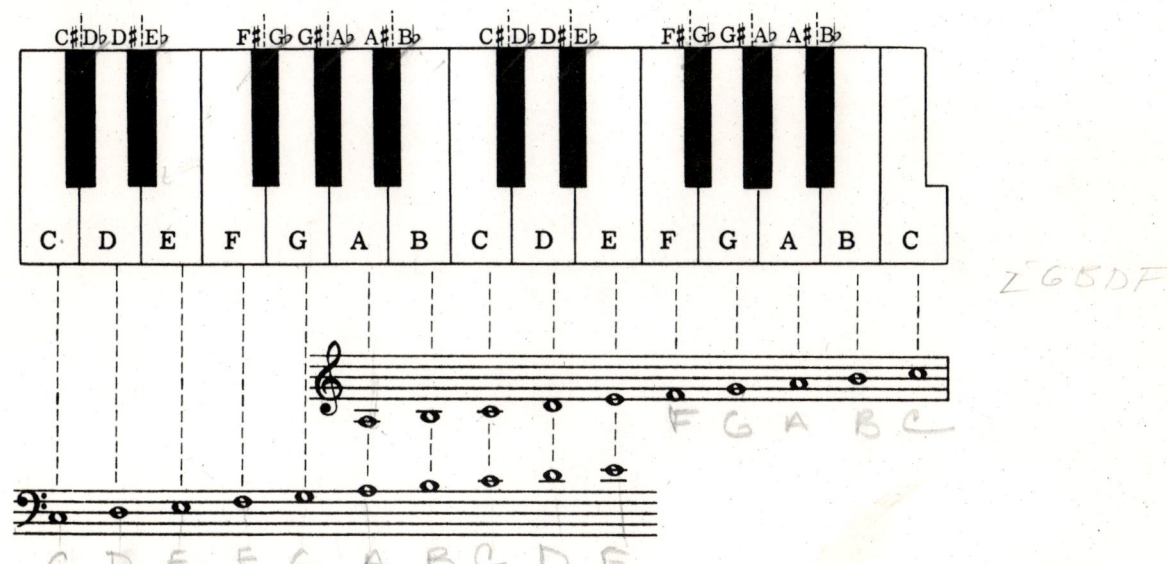

The student will note that there is no black key directly above E or B. Each can be raised by a sharp. Thus E♯ becomes the same pitch as F, and B♯ becomes the same pitch as C. Likewise, C and F may be lowered by a flat becoming the same pitch as B and E respectively. The natural pitches together with the chromatics appear on the great staff as follows:

3

Fundamentals (continued)

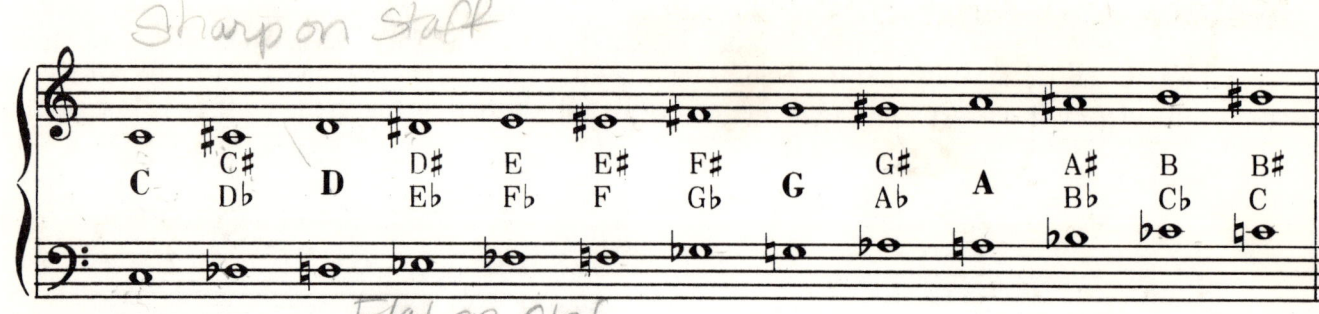

Sharp on staff (handwritten)

Flat on clef (handwritten)

Rhythmic Symbols

The symbols of musical rhythm are notes and rests. The longest value commonly used is the *whole* note (𝅝) and the *whole* rest (▬). Shorter values use appropriate fractional names.

1 whole note
2 half notes
4 quarter notes
8 eighth notes
16 sixteenth notes

A dot added to the note increases the rhythmic value by one half.

dotted half note
dotted quarter note
dotted eighth note
dotted sixteenth note

In instrumental music the stems of eighths and sixteenths are connected by *beams*:

also written
also written

The symbols for rests follow:

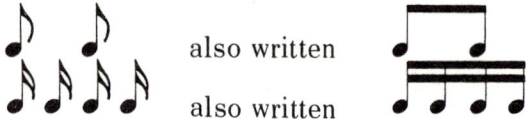

whole -
half -
quarter -
eighth -
sixteenth -

4

Fundamentals (continued)

Meters and Time Signatures

Simple Duple Meter

Simple Triple Meter

Simple Quadruple Meter

Compound Duple Meter

Compound Triple Meter

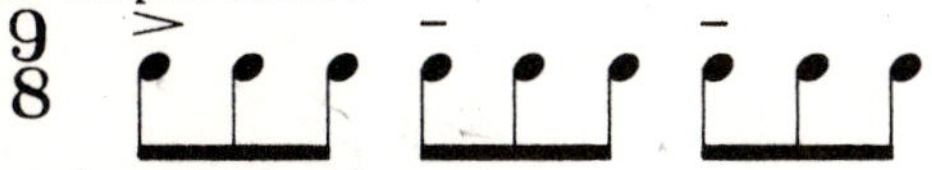

Compound Quadruple Meter

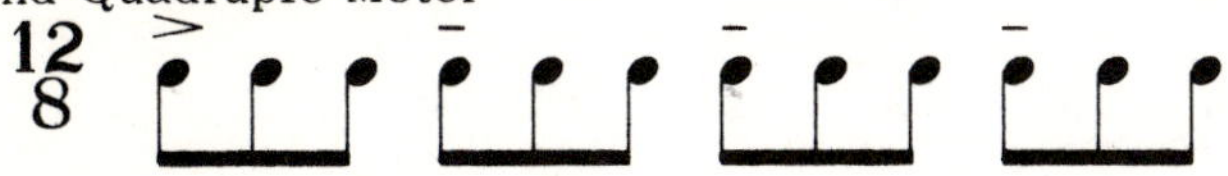

Asymmetric Meters

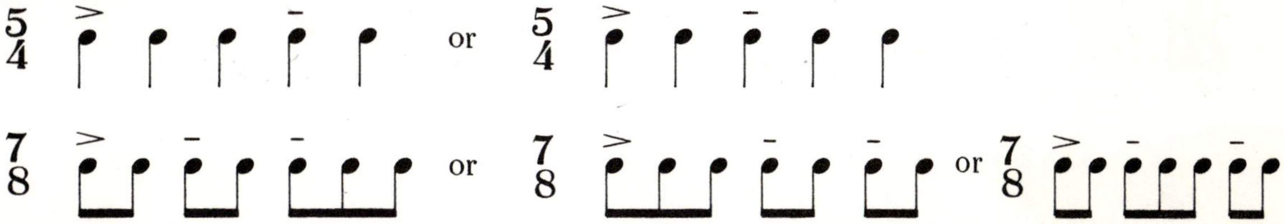

Key Signatures

Major Scales

To facilitate memorizing of fingerings the fourth (4th) finger markings have been circled. Scales may be played separately or together. The authors recommend <u>hands</u> <u>separately</u> for the classroom pianist.

Group A Regular fingering pattern

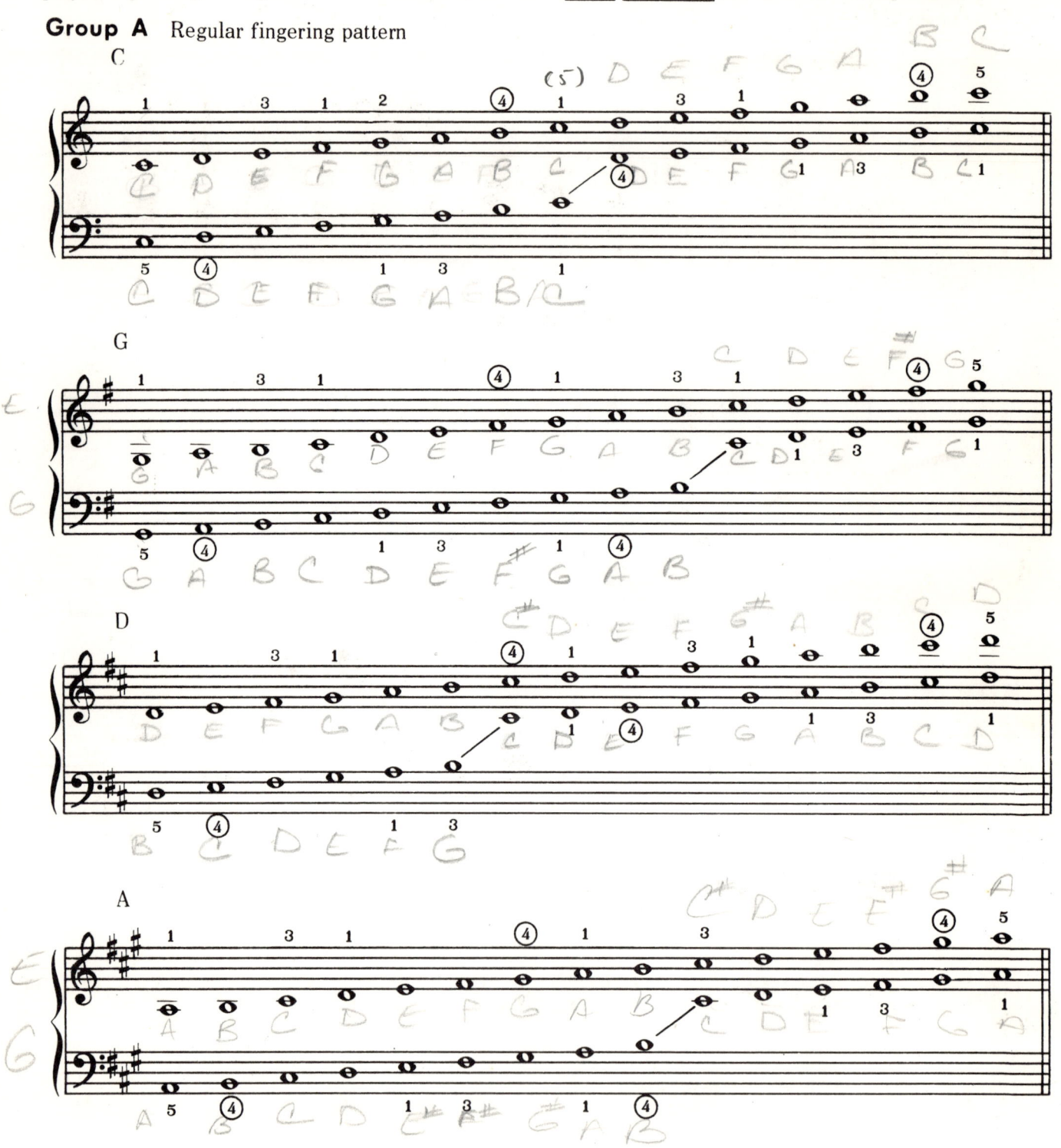

Group B   Fourth finger pattern

Ab

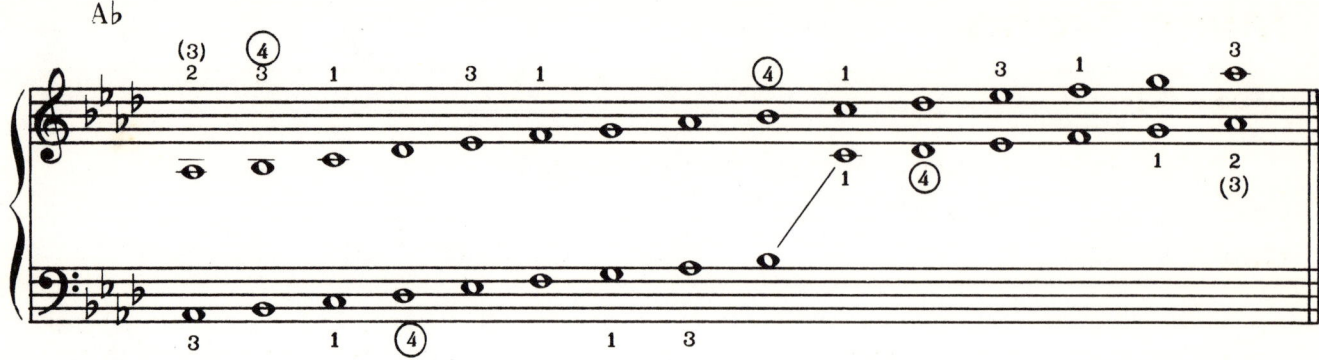

Db

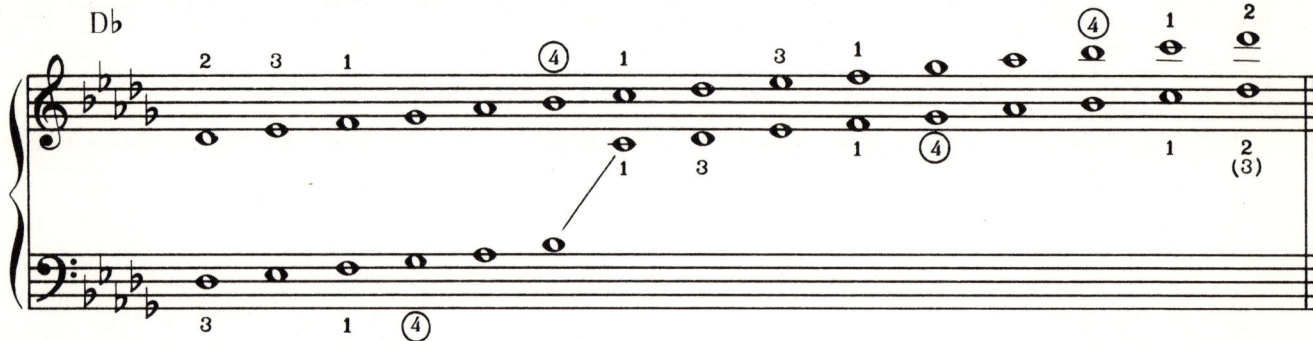

Group C Black key fingering pattern

F#

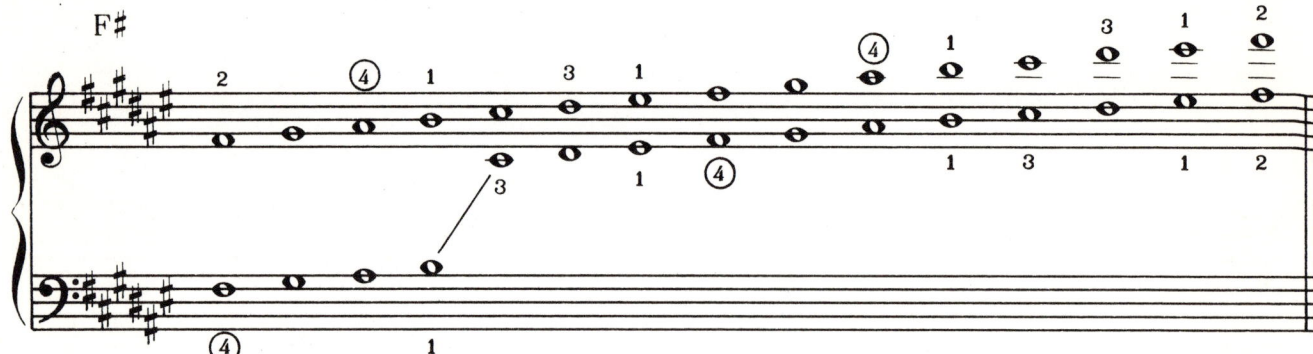

Gb

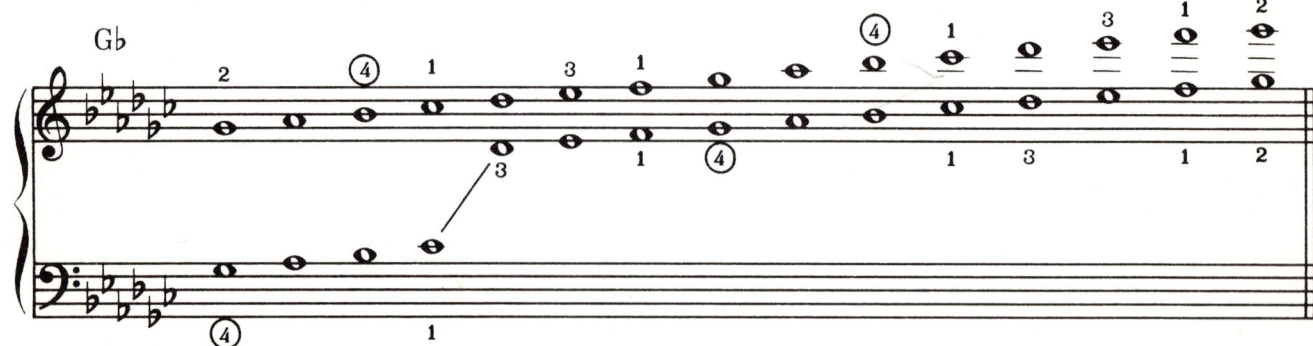

Minor Scales

(Harmonic)

To facilitate memorizing of fingerings the fourth (4th) finger markings have been circled.

Group A

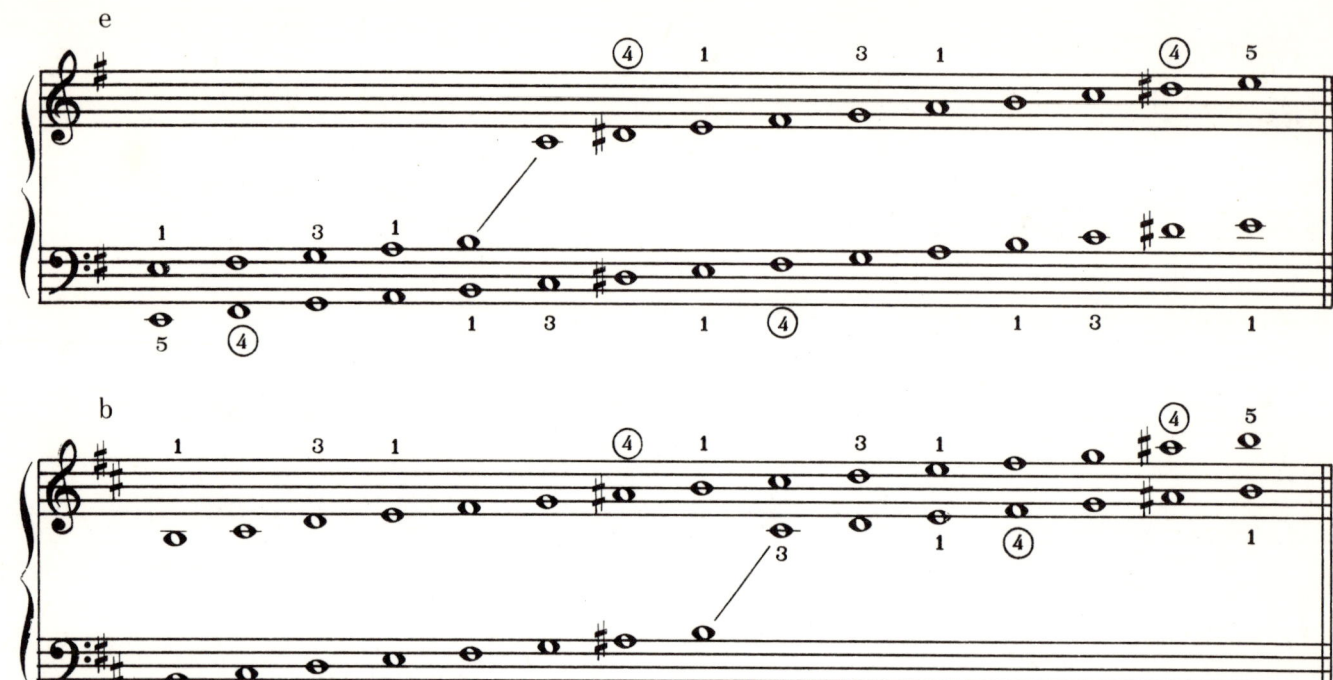

Group B

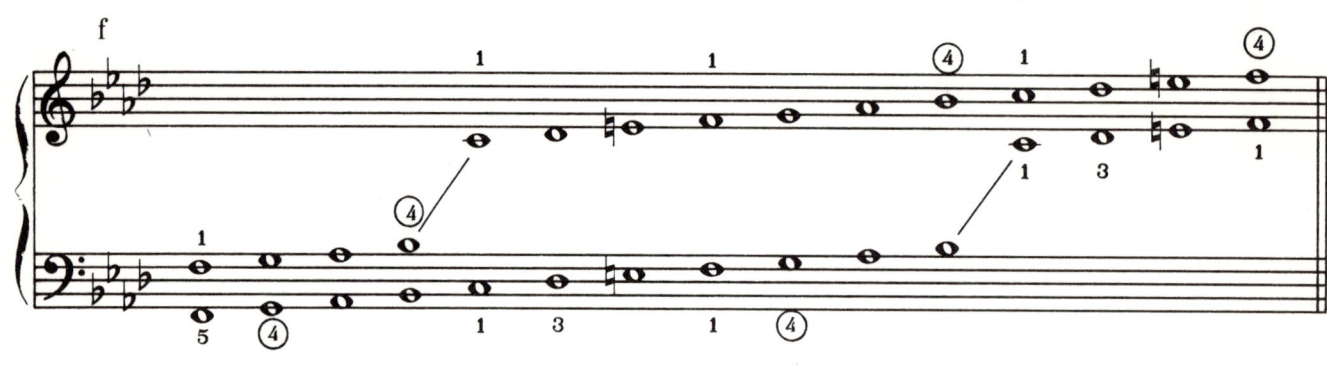

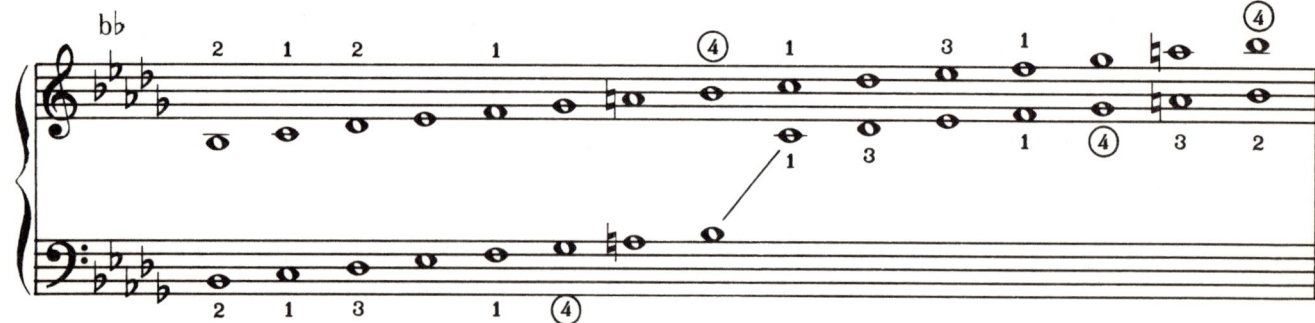

L.H. fingering differs from L.H. B♭ Major.

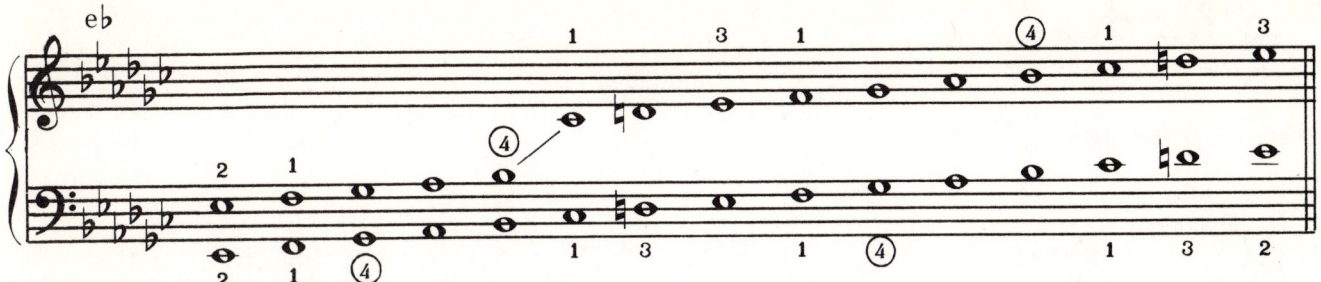

L.H. fingering differs from E♭ Major.

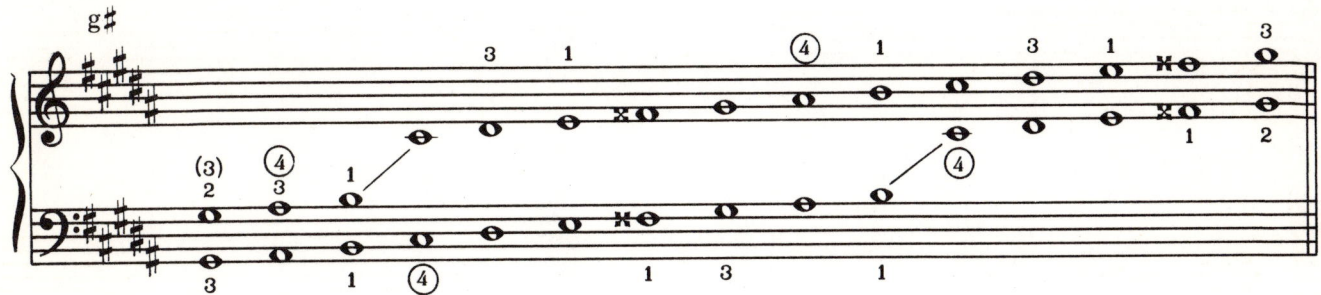

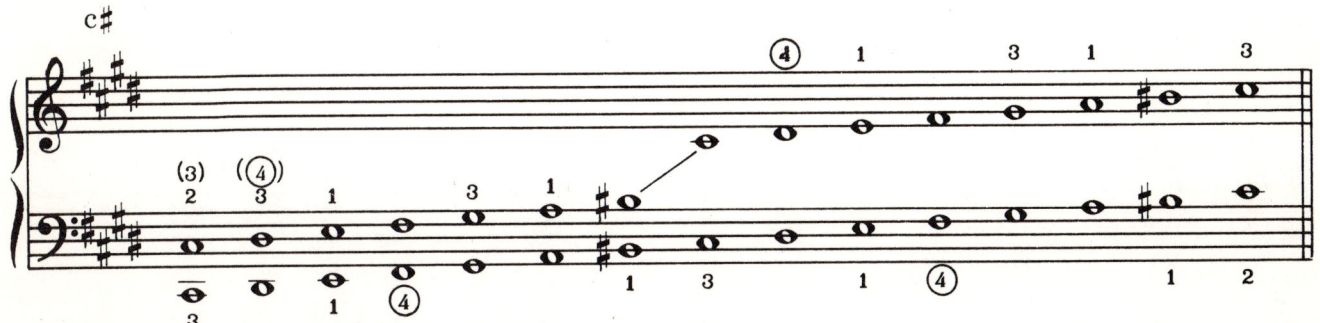

R.H. differs from fingering of D♭ Major.

Group C

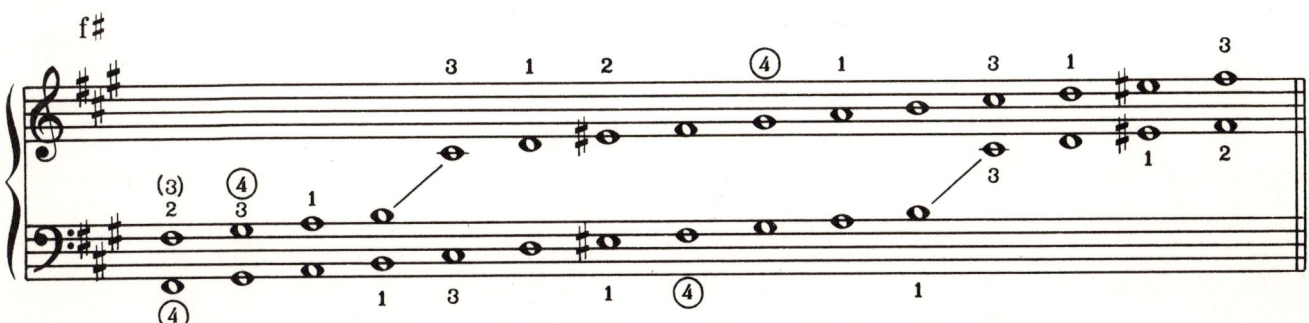

R.H. fingering differs from R.H. of F♯ Major.

The Modes

Medieval Modes

F   Final
D   Dominant

<table>
<tr><td align="center">AUTHENTIC</td><td align="center">PLAGAL</td></tr>
</table>

I. Dorian

II. Hypo-Dorian

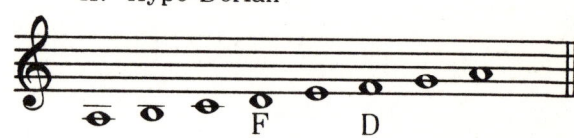

III. Phrygian

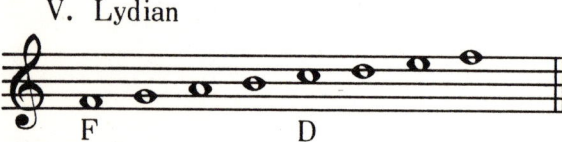

IV. Hypo-Phrygian

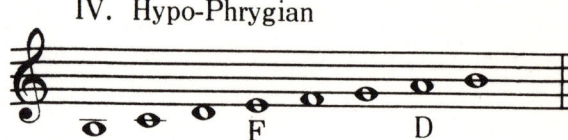

V. Lydian

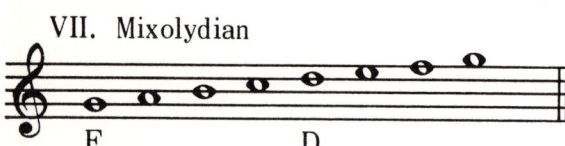

VI. Hypo-Lydian

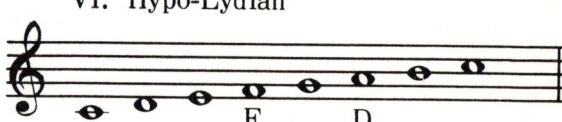

VII. Mixolydian

VIII. Hypo-Mixolydian

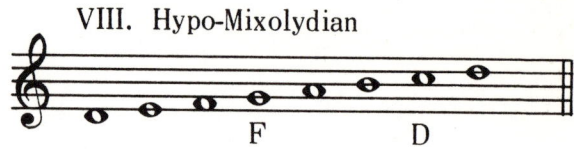

16th Century Additions

IX. Aeolian

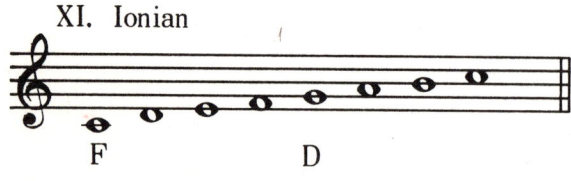

X. Hypo-Aeolian

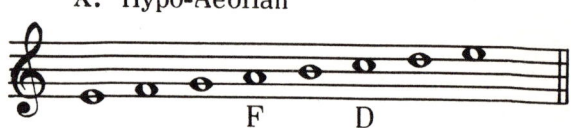

XI. Ionian

XII. Hypo-Ionian

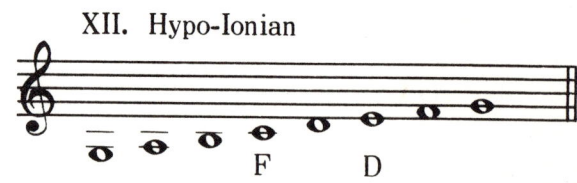

The Ionian Scale is the same as C major.
The Aeolian Scale is the same as a minor (natural form).

The modes are used by many contemporary composers. Among them are Ravel, Bartok, Debussy, Milhaud, Liadow, Bloch, Kabalevsky.

Modal Scales for Practicing

13

The Pentatonic Scale

The Whole—Tone Scale

Notice that the two Whole—Tone scales, starting on "C" and on "Db" are the only Whole—Tone scales possible. Spelling the scale beginning on any tone results in a combination of pitches which formulate the same tones as above.

The Chromatic Scale

When the two Whole—Tone scales are combined they form the Chromatic Scale. Note that the ascending chromatic tones are all sharps; the descending chromatic tones are all flats.

Composers from Bach on have used the Chromatic Scale.

Composers such as Glinka, Liszt, Debussy, Milhaud, and Bartok have used the Whole—Tone scale. Debussy used it to the fullest possibilities.

Techniques

Finger Techniques and Independent Hand Coordination

Play slowly at first. If necessary, hands separately until coordination is attained. Transpose to keys of G, D, A, E and F. Think and feel the shape and direction of the passage in the new key.

c minor

Segment of Phrygian mode (C with four flats). See p. 12 and p. 27.

Segment of Lydian mode (C with one sharp). See p. 12 and p. 27.

Finger Techniques and Independent Hand Coordination

Depress chord silently.
Prepare each tone by lifting finger high.

The following exercises are written in mirror pattern.
Observe that fingerings are identical in both hands.

Independence of Hands:

Note the ABA' Structure. Change from Major to minor by flatting the proper note.

Transpose to D, F and G. Major and minor.

Note the ABA′ structure. Change from Major to minor.

Transpose to G, F, D. Major and minor.

Independence of Hands:
Change from Major to minor.

Transpose to D, F, G. Major and minor.

Independence of Hands and Fingers:
Note canonic, imitative structure. Change from Major to minor.

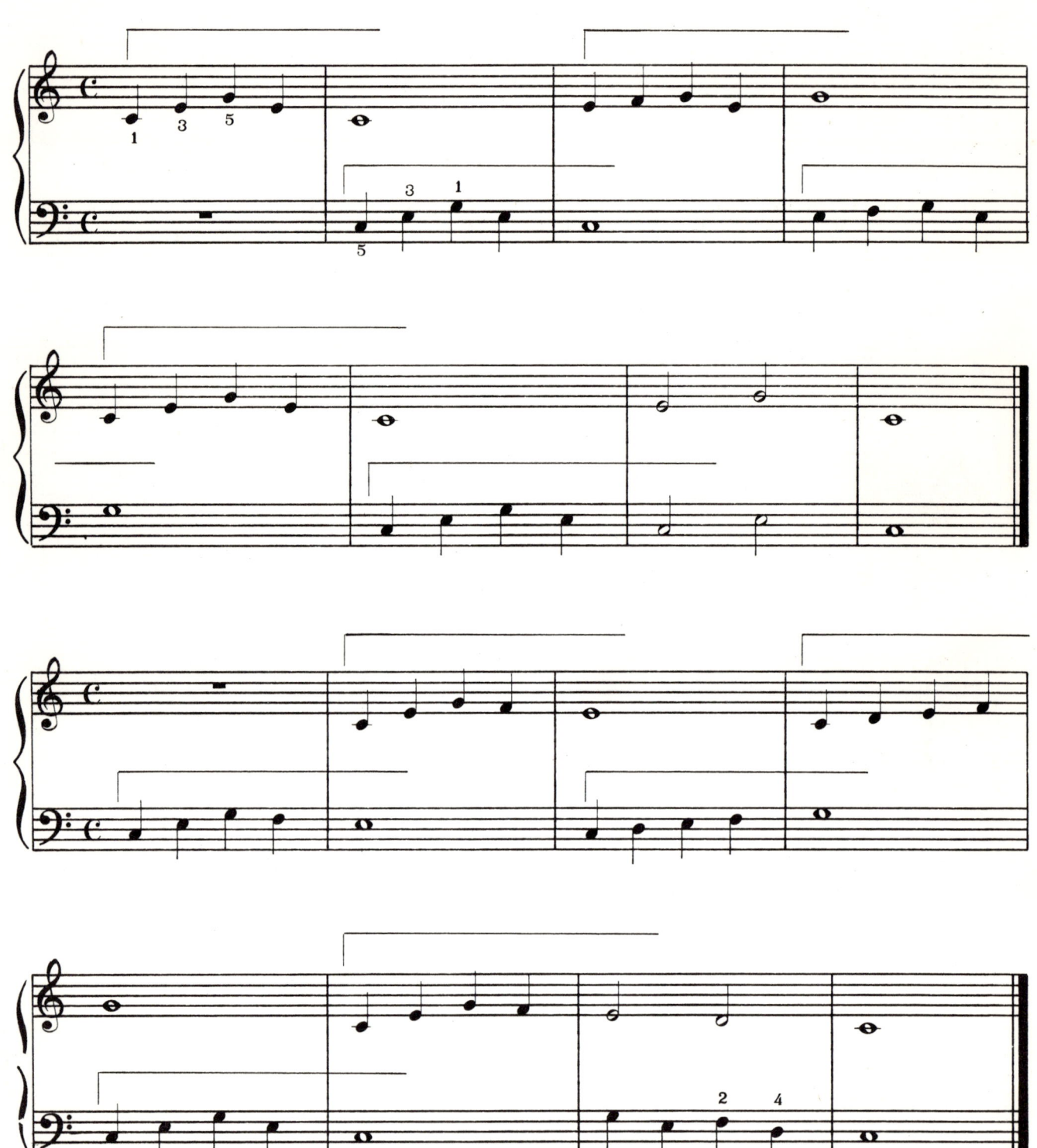

Transpose to G, F, D, A, E. Major and minor.

Chordal Techniques

I.

II.

III.

Staccato Wrist

VICTOR DUVERNOY (1842-1907)

IV.

24

Stacatto Wrist (continued)

Variants of Chordal Exercises:

Apply these variants to chordal drills I, II and III in all keys up to and including four (4) sharps and four (4) flats.

A.

etc.

B.

etc.

25

C.

D.

E.

Scales and Modes

Piano literature contains few examples of scale passages *hands together*. Therefore the practice of playing scales hands together seems questionable, especially for the classroom pianist.

The Major and minor (harmonic) and modal scales with correct fingerings will be found in Section 1.

Playing scales with *proper* fingerings sets up the technique for playing music in a florid idiom.

Suggestions:

Play slowly, hands separately, until fingerings are well established. As *proficiency develops extend the range to four octaves and gradually* increase the speed. Playing too fast too soon can be discouraging. When coordination is well established speed will come.

It goes without saying that techniques in the most frequently used keys should be established first. After the scales of C, G, and F are mastered extend the range to more remote keys.

Scales can be grouped by similarity of fingering and mastery of scales can be facilitated by establishing fingering habits by grouping practice. Here are the groupings:

Group A. Regular Fingering Pattern

Right hand: 123, 1234, 123, 1234, etc. Applies to scales of C, G, D, A, E, B
Left hand: 54321, 321, 4321, 321, etc. Applies to scales of C, G, D, A, E, F
    It is suggested that this group be mastered first.

Group B. Fourth Finger Pattern

Right hand: 4th finger goes on first flat (B♭). Applies to F, B♭, E♭, A♭, D♭
Left hand: 4th finger goes on last flat in key signature. Applies to B♭, E♭, A♭, D♭

Group C. Black Key Fingering Pattern

Fingers 2 and 3 go on the two black keys
Fingers 2, 3, and 4 go on the three black keys
    Applies (both hands) to Gb, Cb, B, F♯, and C♯.
    The modes, which are found in medieval music, consist of selections of tones arranged as scales. The various modes on the white keys of the piano follow:
    Dorian: d to d′
    Phrygian: e to e′
    Lydian: f to f′
    Mixolydian: g to g′
    Aeolian: a to a′
    Some musicians relate the modes to the scale of C and add key signatures to secure the proper intervals between the tones, as follows:
    Dorian: C with two flats
    Phrygian: C with four flats
    Lydian: C with one sharp
    Mixolydian: C with one flat
    Aeolian: C with three flats
    In writing, modal music composers may start on any note and devise the desired modal scale by means of sharps or flats to achieve the proper interval relationships. Music composed in this fashion is said to be "mode transposed." i.e., "dorian transposed." Examples of this will be seen in the modal pieces found elsewhere in this book.
    Modal scales will be found in Section 1.
    Examples of pieces in the modes will be found on pp. 75–93

Keyboard Harmony

Harmonization in Major

Figured Bass

When a note other than the root of a chord appears in the bass part the chord is said to be inverted. The system of marking inverted chords is called figured bass with figures under the bass note designating the various intervals of the chord. Here are the figures of the inversions used in this book:

Triads
A "6" indicates the first inversion with the *third* in the bass
A "$^6_4$" indicates the second inversion with the *fifth* in the bass

Seventh Chords
A "7" indicates the chord with root in the bass
A "$^6_5$" indicates the first inversion with the *third* in the bass
A "$^4_3$" indicates the second inversion with the *fifth* in the bass
A "2" indicates the third inversion with the *seventh* in the bass

Preliminary Chord Drill

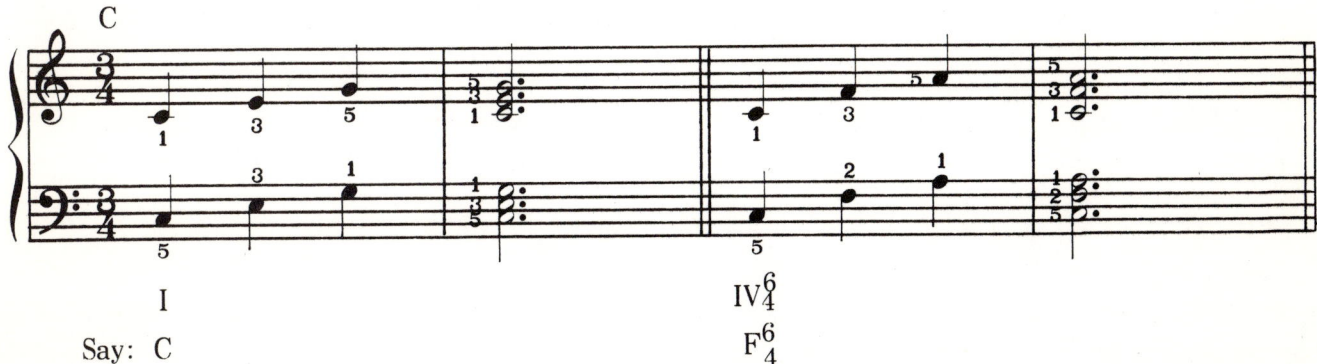

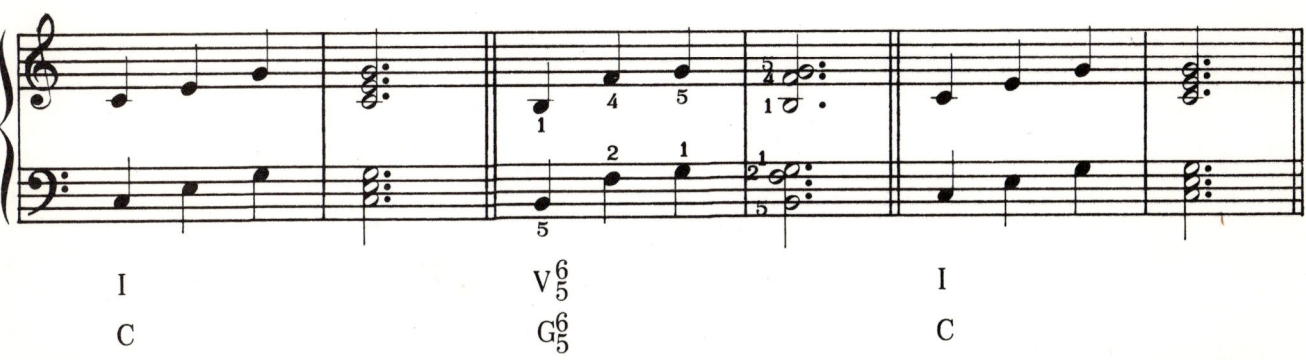

Write and play, as illustrated, in keys of G, B♭, D, E♭, A, E.

Say: F   B♭$^6_4$

I   IV$^6_4$

F   C$^6_5$ F

I   V$^6_5$ I

<u>Scale</u> <u>of</u> <u>Triads</u>   Use damper pedal after each chord (Syncopated Pedal)

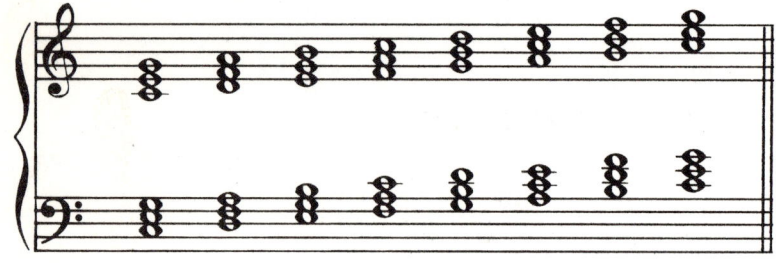

<u>The</u> <u>Major</u> <u>Scale</u> <u>Harmonized</u>   Use damper pedal after each chord

I V I V$^4_3$ I^6 IV vii^{o6} I   iii IV I ii^6 I$^6_4$ V$_7$ I

Say: C G C G$^4_3$ C^6 F b^{o6} C   e F C d^6 C$^6_4$ G$_7$ C

Hot Cross Buns

FOLK SONG

Mary Had a Little Lamb

FOLK SONG

Dancing Song

BOHEMIAN FOLK SONG

Sur Le Pont

FOLK SONG

Chord drill:

Skip to My Lou

AMERICAN FOLK SONG

Transpose and play in the following keys: C, D, B♭, A, E♭, A♭.

Oh! Susanna

Chord drill:

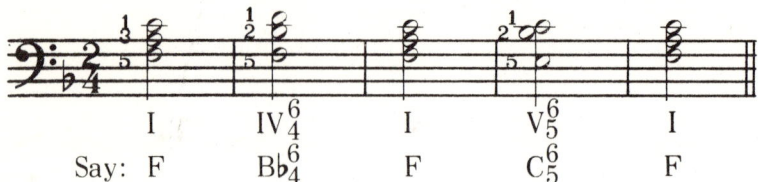

$$I \quad IV_4^6 \quad I \quad V_5^6 \quad I$$

Say: F $\quad$ Bb$_4^6$ $\quad$ F $\quad$ C$_5^6$ $\quad$ F

Block chords:

STEPHEN C. FOSTER 1826–1864

$$I \qquad I \qquad I \qquad V_5^6$$

Say: F $\qquad$ F $\qquad$ F $\qquad$ C$_5^6$

$$I \qquad I \qquad I \quad V_5^6 \qquad I$$

F $\qquad$ F $\qquad$ F $\quad$ C$_5^6$ $\qquad$ F

$$IV_4^6 \qquad IV_4^6 \qquad I \qquad V_5^6$$

Bb$_4^6$ $\qquad$ Bb$_4^6$ $\qquad$ F $\qquad$ C$_5^6$

$$I \qquad I \qquad I \quad V_5^6 \qquad I$$

F $\qquad$ F $\qquad$ F $\quad$ C$_5^6$ $\qquad$ F

Oh! Susanna

STEPHEN C. FOSTER (1826-1864)

Oh! Susanna

Chord drill:

STEPHEN C. FOSTER 1826–1864

Syncopated Accompaniment:

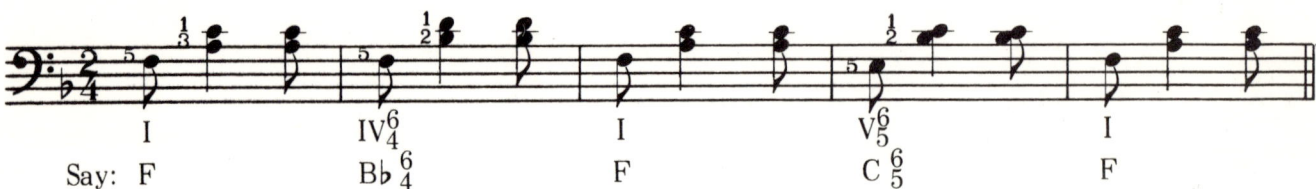

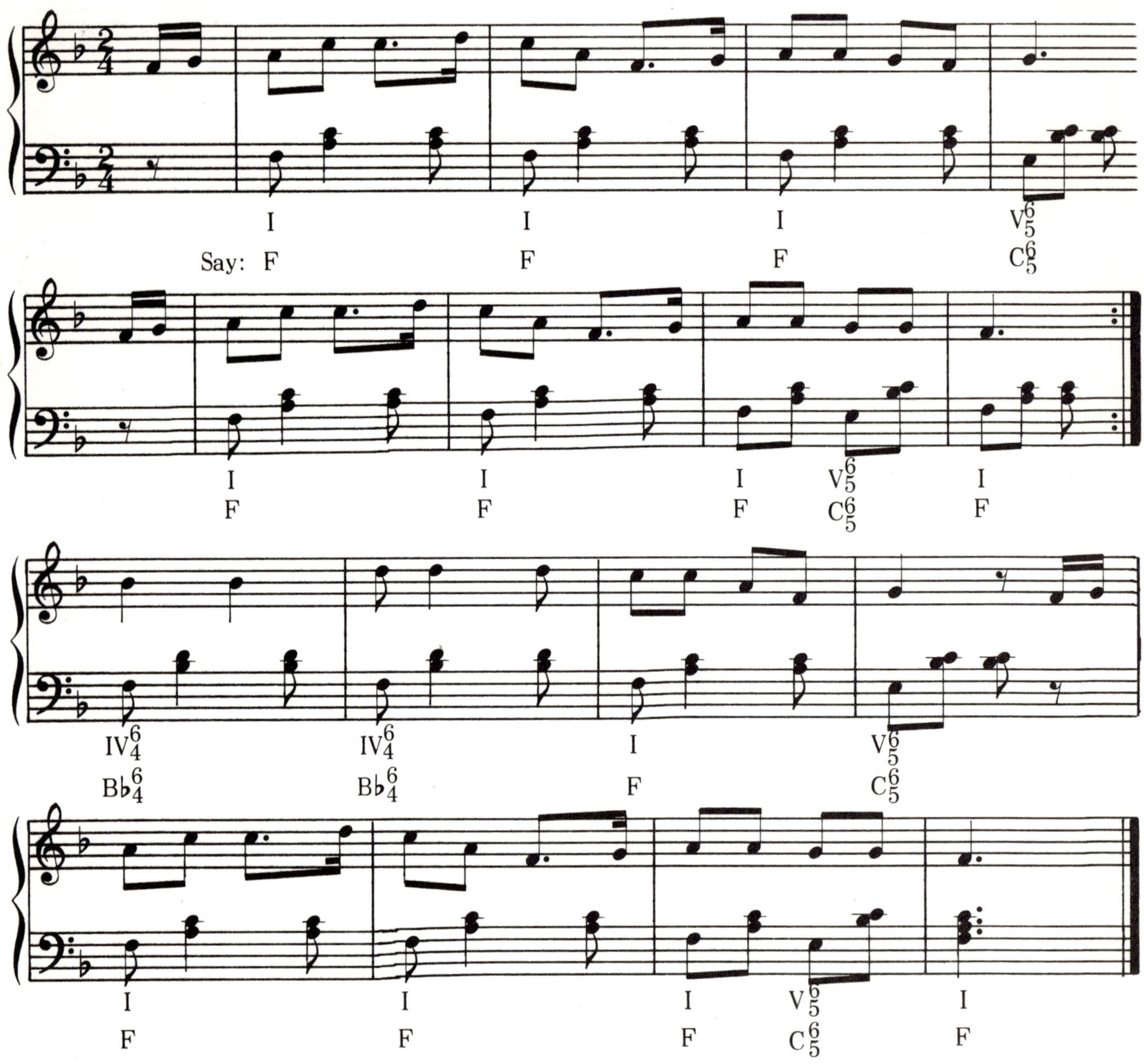

Augustine

Chord drill:

GERMAN FOLK SONG

Bouncing Bass:

Say:

Transpose and play in the keys of F, C, D, Bb, A, Eb, E.

Using the accompaniment styles given in "Skip To My Lou," "Oh! Susanna" and "Augustine" harmonize the following:

Sleep, Baby Sleep

I, V₇ Chords:

OLD SONG

Transpose to various keys.

Come Away, Sang the River

I, V₇ Chords:

GERMAN FOLK SONG

Transpose to various keys.

Who Are You?

I, V₇ Chords:

GERMAN FOLK SONG

Transpose to various keys.

My Pony

GERMAN FOLK SONG

I, V₇ Chords:

Transpose to various keys.

Jack-in-the-Pulpit

GERMAN FOLK SONG

I, V₇ Chords:

Transpose to various keys.

The Farmer

GERMAN FOLK SONG

I, V₇ Chords:

Transpose to various keys.

This Old Man

GERMAN FOLK SONG

I, V₇ Chords:

Transpose to various keys.

Cindy

AMERICAN FOLK SONG

I, IV, V₇ Chords (block chords as indicated by x):

Play also with bouncing bass. Transpose to various keys.

Gretel Pastetel

Chord drill:

GERMAN FOLK SONG

I	IV^6_4	I	V_6	V^6_5	I
Say: F	B♭ $^6_5$	F	C_6	C $^6_5$	F

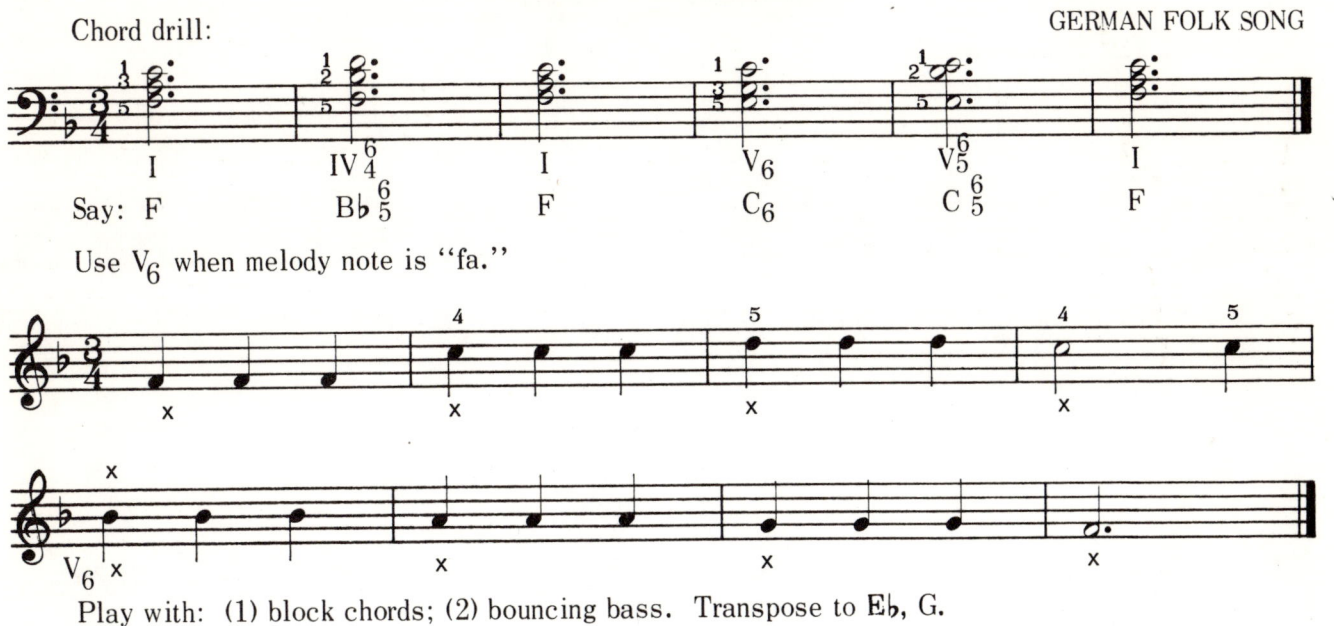

Use V_6 when melody note is "fa."

Play with: (1) block chords; (2) bouncing bass. Transpose to E♭, G.

The Troubadour

Chord drill:

OLD SONG

I	V^6_5	I	IV^6_4	I	V_6	I
Say: E♭	B♭ $^6_5$	E♭	A♭ $^6_4$	E♭	B♭$_6$	E♭

Play with: (1) block chords; (2) bouncing bass. Transpose to D, E, F.

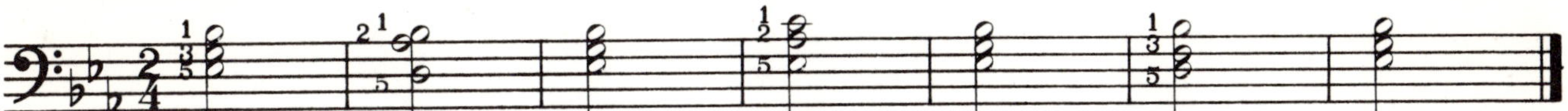

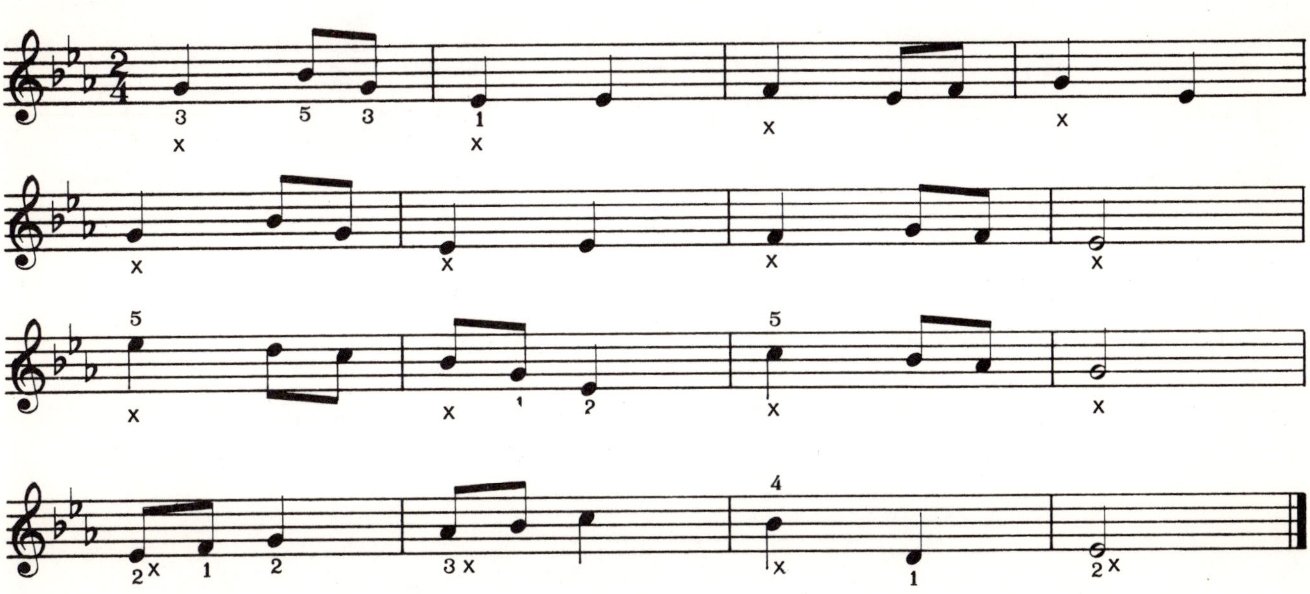

German Folk Song

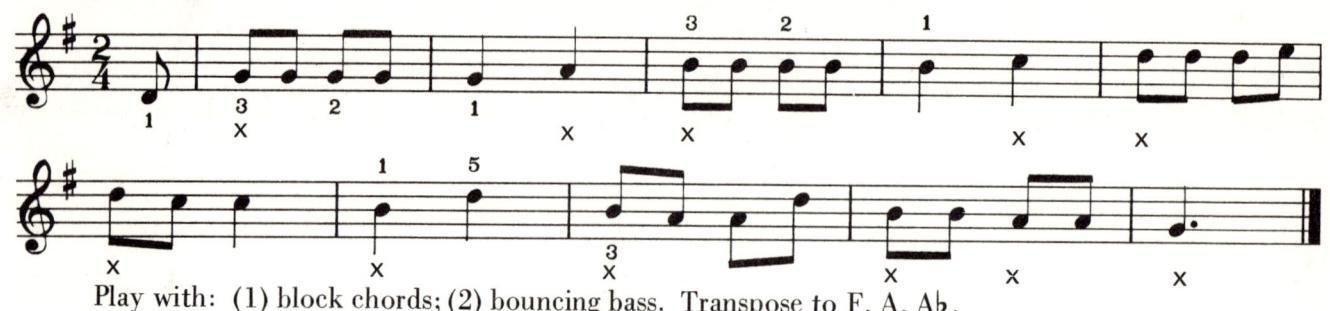

Play with: (1) block chords; (2) bouncing bass. Transpose to F, A, A♭.

Schubert Melody

English Folk Song

I, IV, V Chords

Block chords indicated by x; Play bouncing bass also.

44

Musieu Bainjo

I, V Chords

Swedish Folk Song

I, IV, V Chords

English Folk Song

I, IV, V Chords

45

Substitution Chart

1. ii⁶ can be substituted for IV in some harmonizations. Both chords have subdominant function.

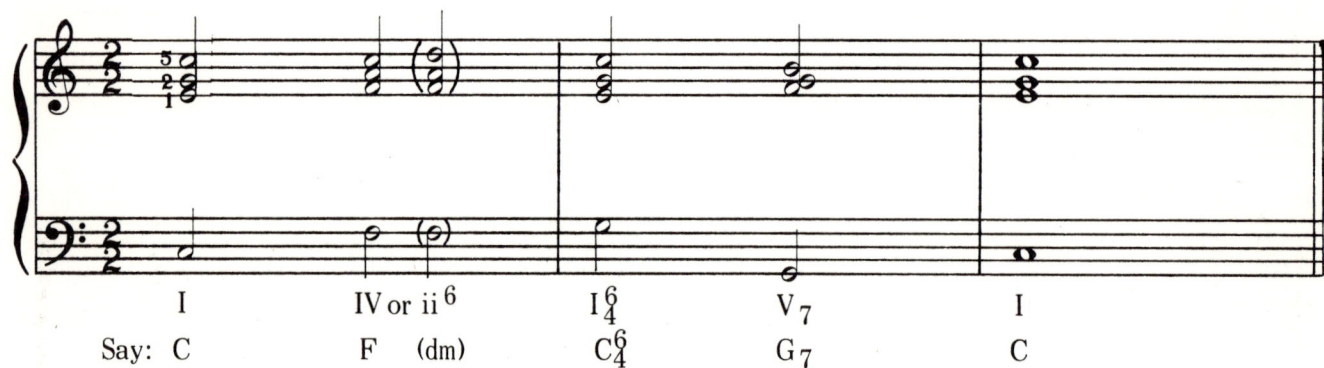

2. vi can be substituted for I in some harmonizations. Both chords have tonic function.

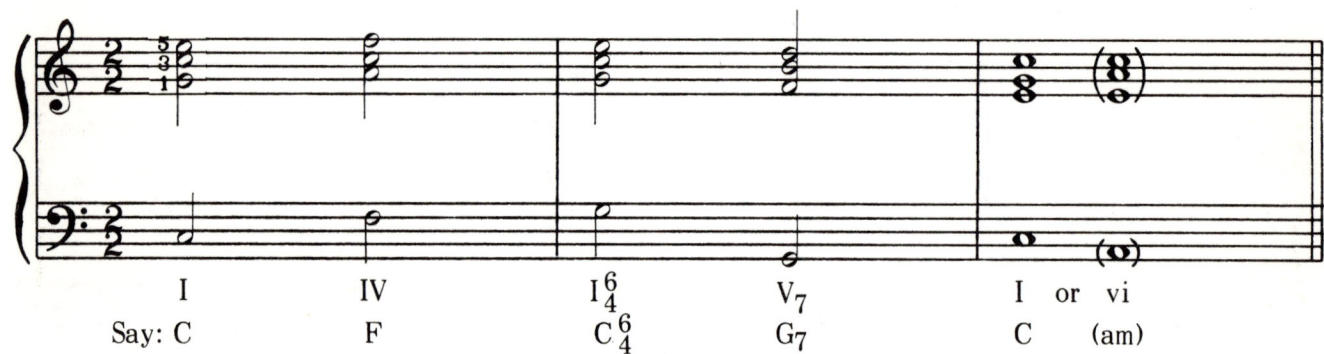

3. vi can also follow I. ii⁶ can also follow IV.

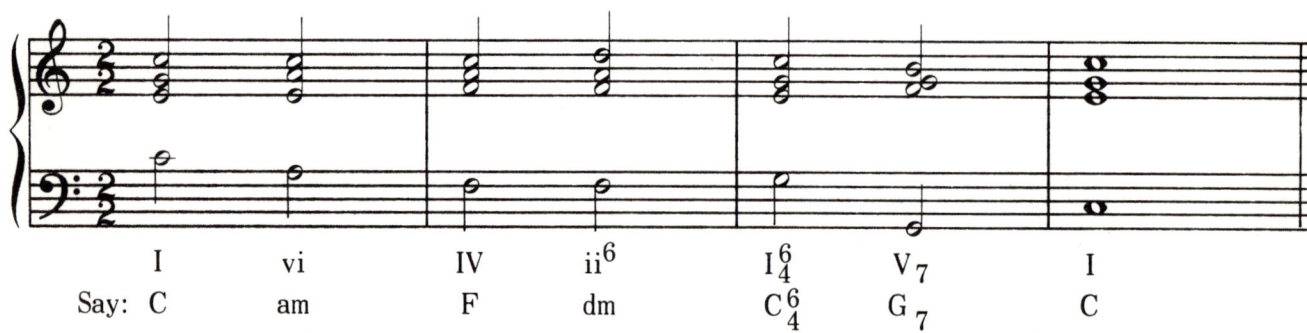

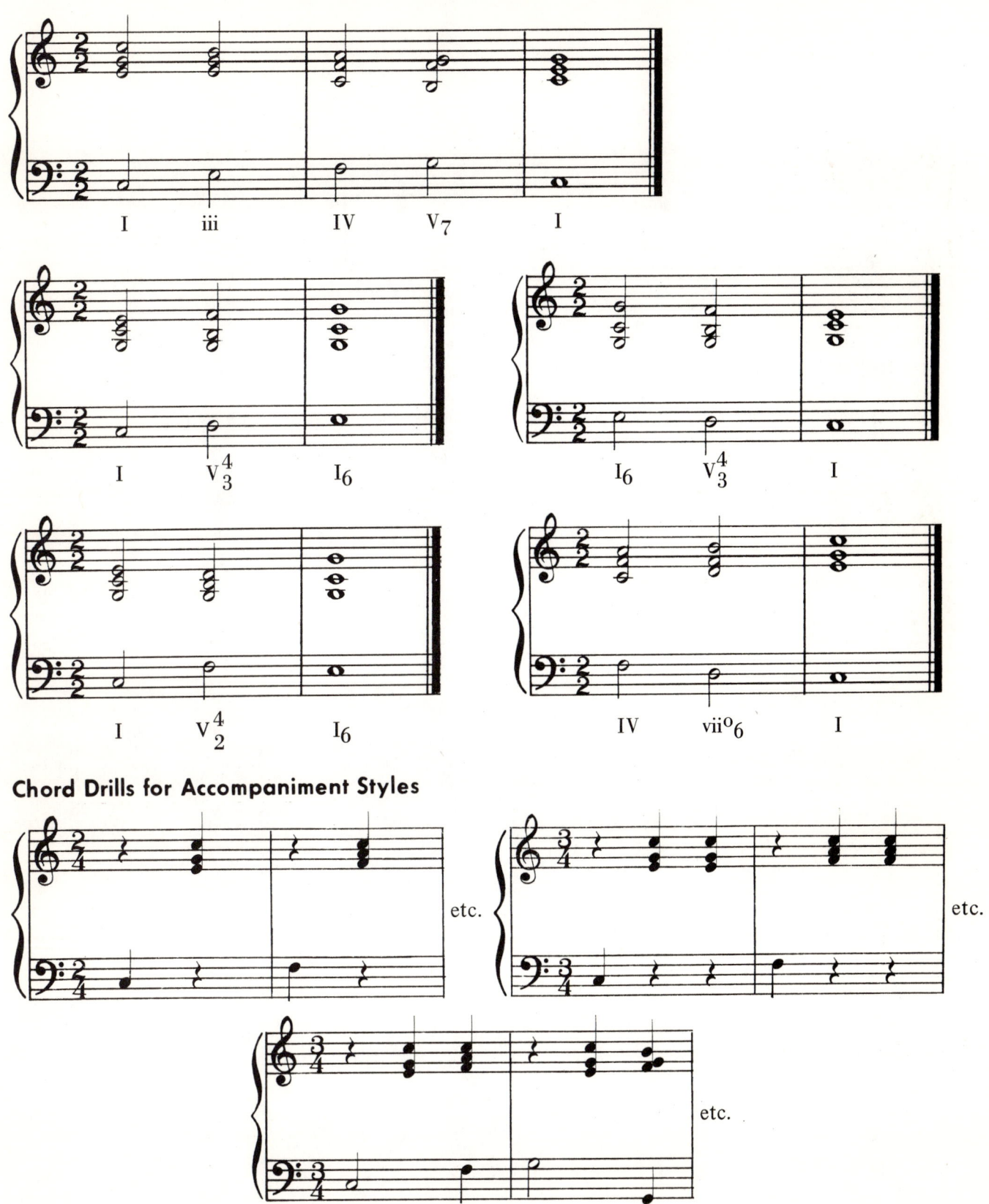

Chord Drills for Accompaniment Styles

etc.

etc.

etc.

Transpose and practice these drills in keys of F, D. E♭, G.

Sing SWANEE RIVER while playing an accompaniment in the following style:

Songs to Play by Ear

Using the chords from the preceding progressions, accompany the following songs by ear.

1. Kum Ba Yah . . . . C . . . . $\frac{3}{4}$ meter

2. Happy Birthday . . . . F . . . . $\frac{3}{4}$ meter

3. Swanee River . . . . D . . . . $\frac{4}{4}$ meter

4. Old MacDonald . . . . E . . . . $\frac{2}{4}$ meter

5. Sing Your Way Home . . . . G . . . . $\frac{3}{4}$ meter

6. Farmer in the Dell . . . . G . . . . $\frac{6}{8}$ meter

7. O Dear, What Can the Matter Be . . . . D . . . . $\frac{6}{8}$ meter

8. Jacob's Ladder . . . . D . . . . $\frac{4}{4}$ meter

9. Dona Nobis Pacem . . . . F . . . . $\frac{3}{4}$ meter

10. La Cucaracha . . . . F . . . . $\frac{3}{4}$ meter

11. Kookaburra . . . . D . . . . $\frac{2}{4}$ meter

12. The Holly and the Ivy . . . . F . . . . $\frac{3}{4}$ meter

13. The Keel Row . . . . F . . . . $\frac{2}{4}$ meter

14. Camptown Races . . . . D . . . . $\frac{2}{4}$ meter

CADENCES: FIRST SET
(Major Keys)

Position of the 5th.

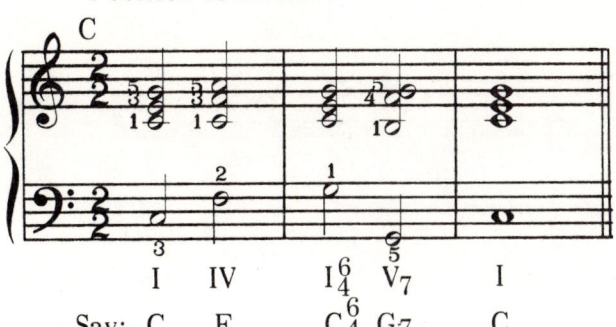

	I	IV	I$_4^6$	V$_7$	I
Say:	C	F	C$_4^6$	G$_7$	C

Write and play ($\half$ = 72).

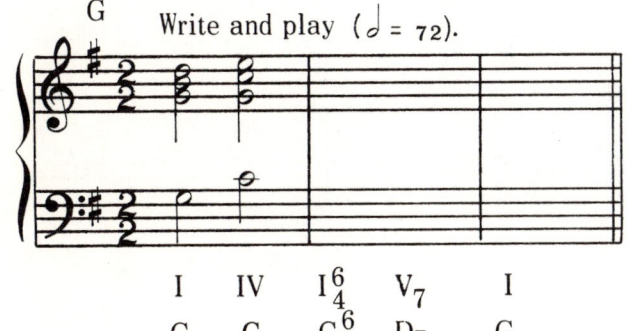

I	IV	I$_4^6$	V$_7$	I
G	C	G$_4^6$	D$_7$	G

I	IV	I$_4^6$	V$_7$	I
F	B♭	F$_4^6$	C$_7$	F

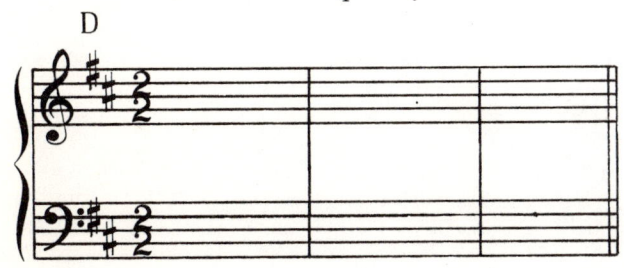

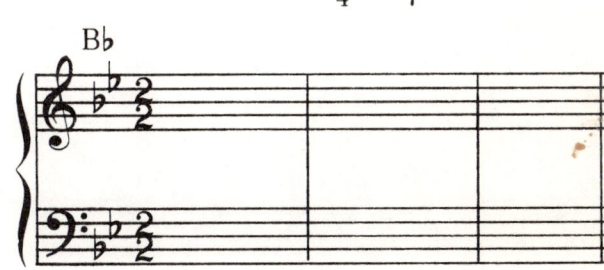

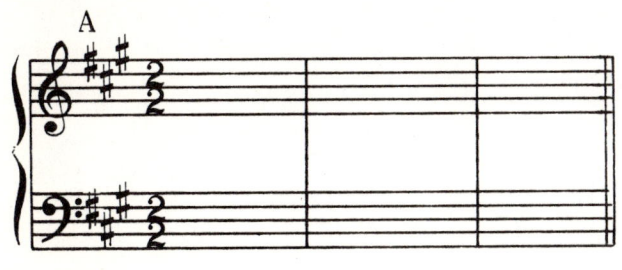

49

Position of the 8ve:

I   IV   I$^6_4$ V$_7$ I

Say: C   F   C$^6_4$ G$_7$ C

G Write and play ($\bf{\downarrow}$ = 72).

I   IV   I$^6_4$ V$_7$ I

G   C   G$^6_4$ D$_7$ G

I   IV   I$^6_4$ V$_7$ I

F   B♭   F$^6_4$ C$_7$ F

D

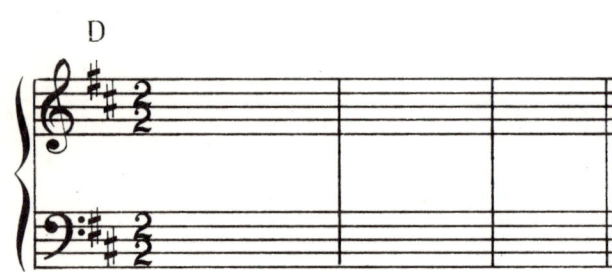

B♭

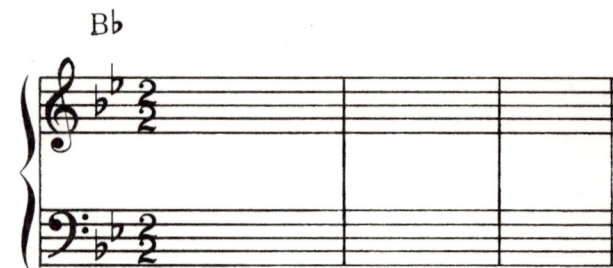

A

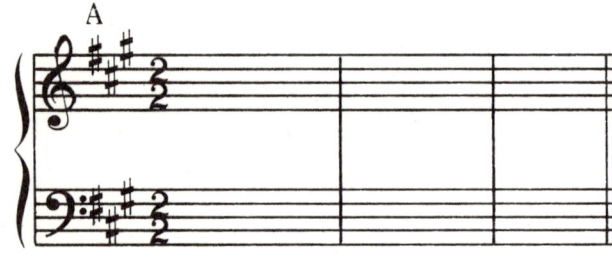

E♭

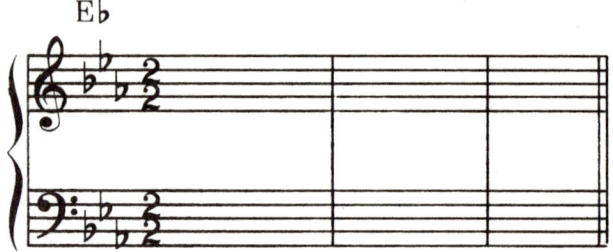

E

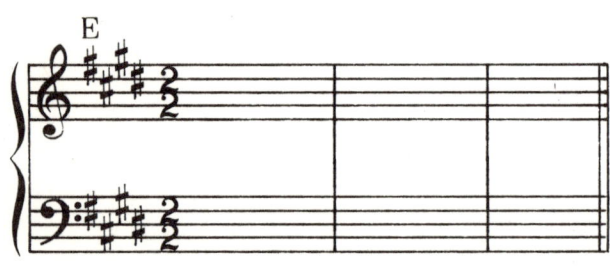

A♭

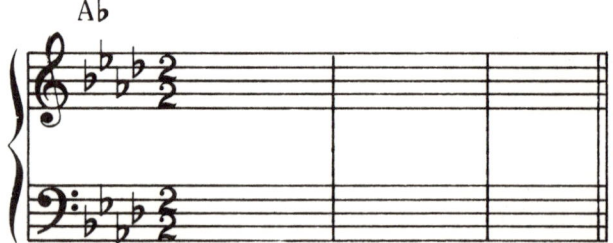

Position of the 3rd:

	I	IV	I$_4^6$	V$_7$	I
Say:	C	F	C$_4^6$	G$_7$	C

Write and play ($\half = 72$).

I	IV	I$_4^6$	V$_7$	I
G	C	G$_4^6$	D$_7$	G

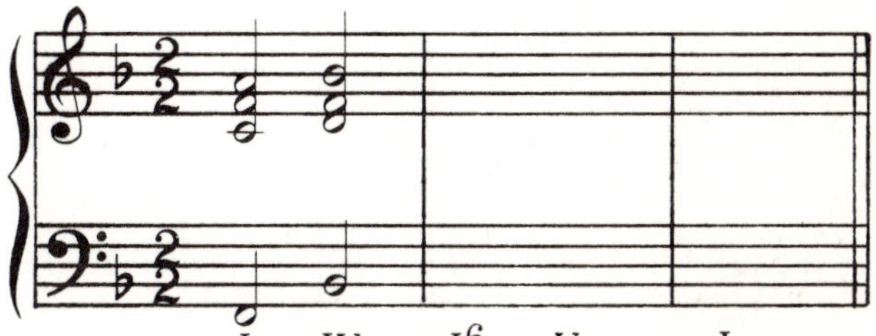

I	IV	I$_4^6$	V$_7$	I
F	B♭	F$_4^6$	C$_7$	F

D

B♭

A

E♭

E

A♭

Harmonization in Minor

Preliminary Chord Drill:

C Minor

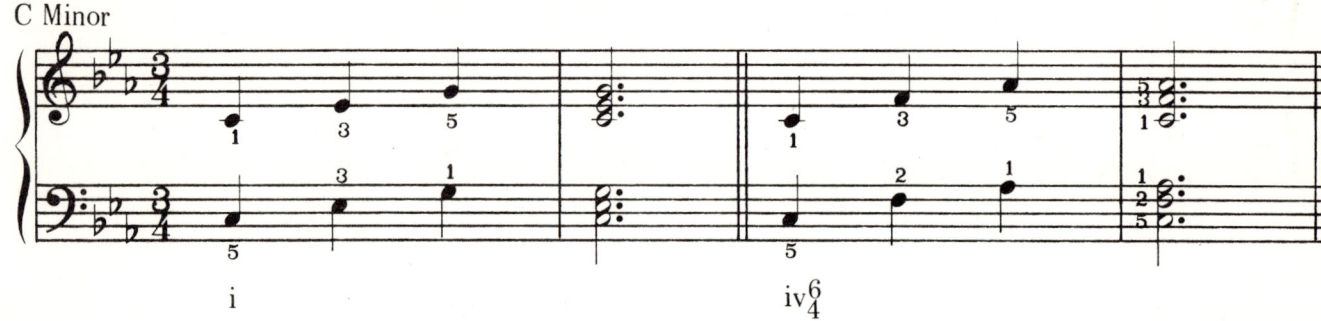

i   iv$^6_4$

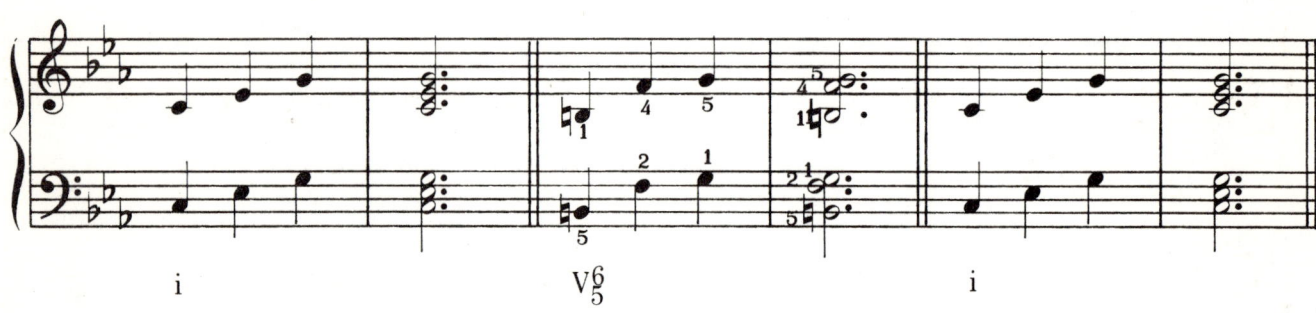

i   V$^6_5$ i

Write and play, as illustrated, in keys of d, e, g, b, f minor.

D minor

i   iv$^6_4$

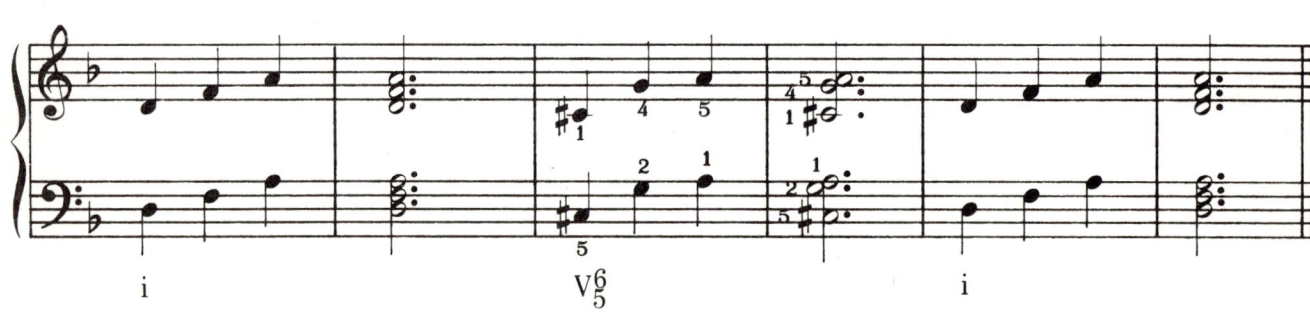

i   V$^6_5$ i

DIATONIC PROGRESSIONS IN MINOR

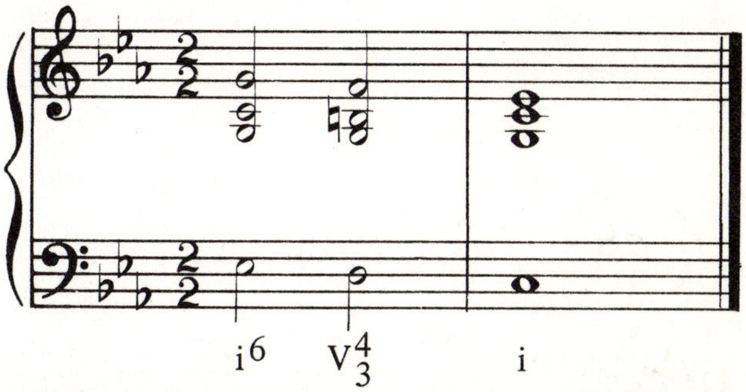

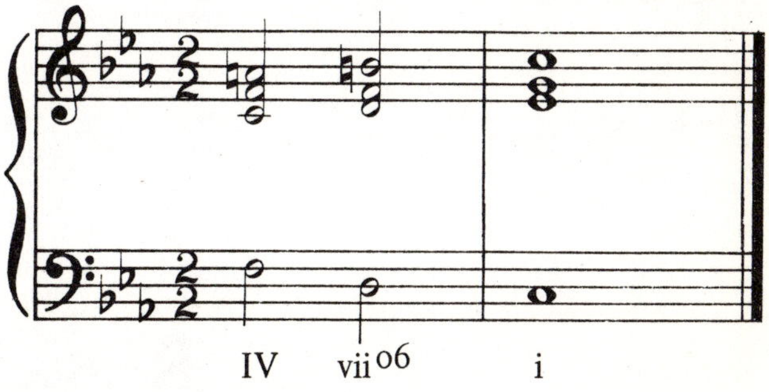

i   III   iv   V$_7$ i

i   V$_3^4$ i^6

i^6 V$_3^4$ i

i   V$_2^4$ i^6

IV   vii^{o6} i

Scale of Triads   Use damper pedal after each chord

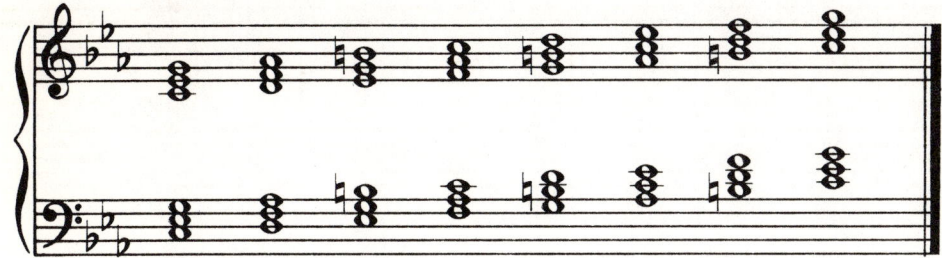

The Minor Scale (Melodic Form) Harmonized
Use damper pedal after each chord

i   V   i   V$_3^4$ i^6 IV   vii^{o6} i   III   iv   i   ii^{o6} i$_4^6$ V^7 i

53

Hatikvah

ISRAEL

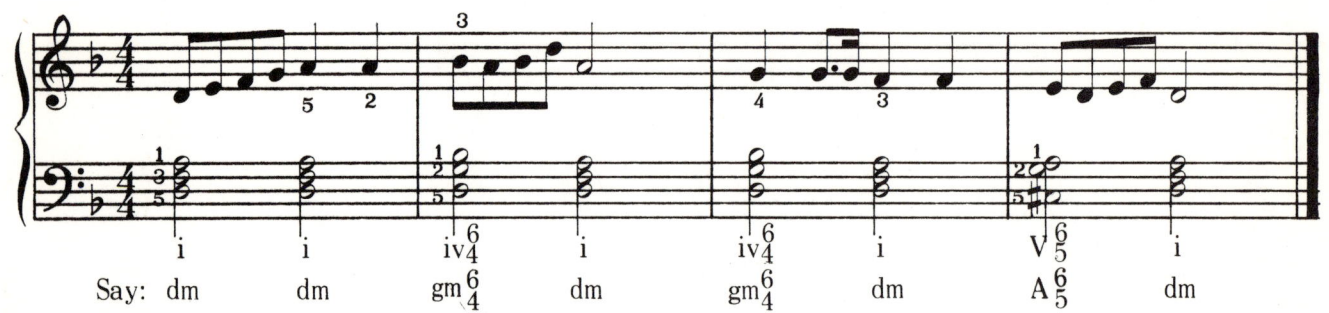

Write and play in the keys of a, g, b, c

Russian Folk Song

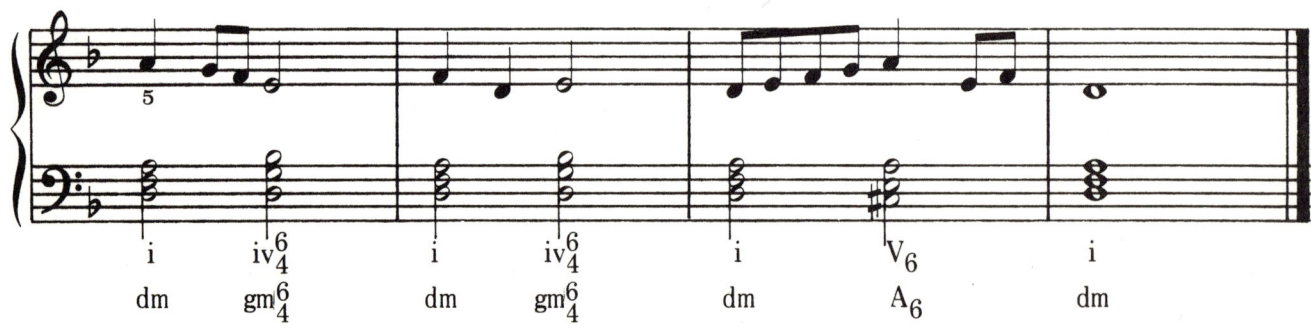

Russian Folk Song

Transpose, write and play in the following keys: a, g, b, c, f.

Chord drill:

The Pedlar

(Chords indicated by x)

Play with: (1) block chords, (2) bouncing bass.

etc.

Transpose to cm, em.

55

God, Our Loving Father

Chord drill:

FINNISH MELODY

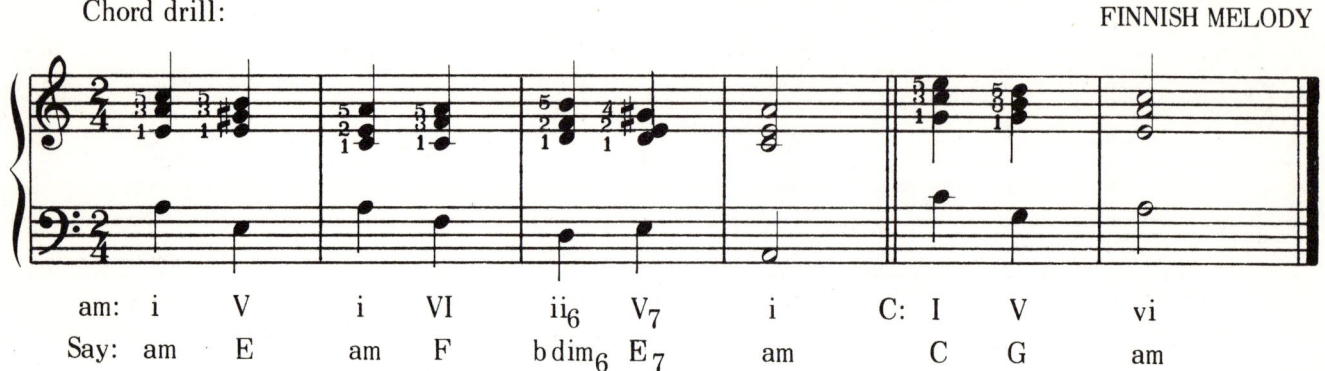

am: i   V   i   VI   ii$_6$ V$_7$ i   C: I V   vi

Say: am E   am F   b dim$_6$ E$_7$ am   C G   am

Slow

Play with right hand block chords. Transpose to keys of cm, gm.

Using the left—hand block chord style harmonize the following:

Poor Man, Poor Man

HUNGARIAN FOLK SONG

Evening Greeting

Moderato

GERMAN FOLK SONG

As I Was Walking

Moderato

FRENCH FOLK SONG

Carol

Fast

FRENCH

Musette

Allegretto

FRENCH

Fine

D. S. al Fine

Russian Folk Song

Swedish Folk Song

Russian Folk Song

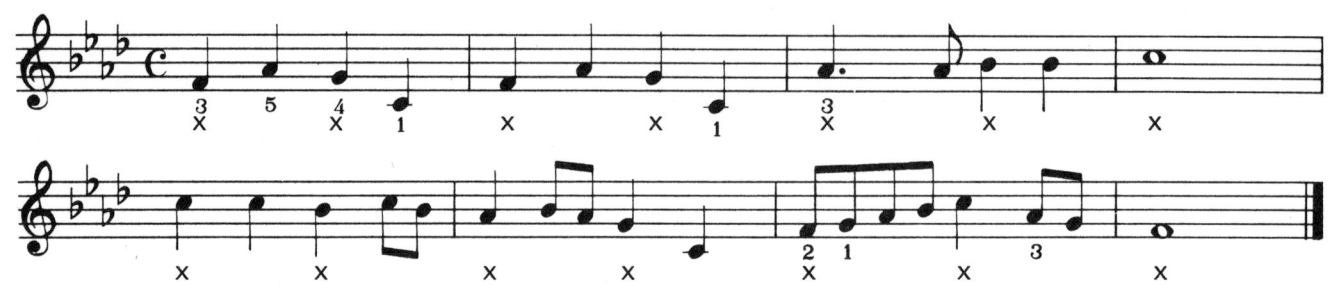

Czech Folk Song

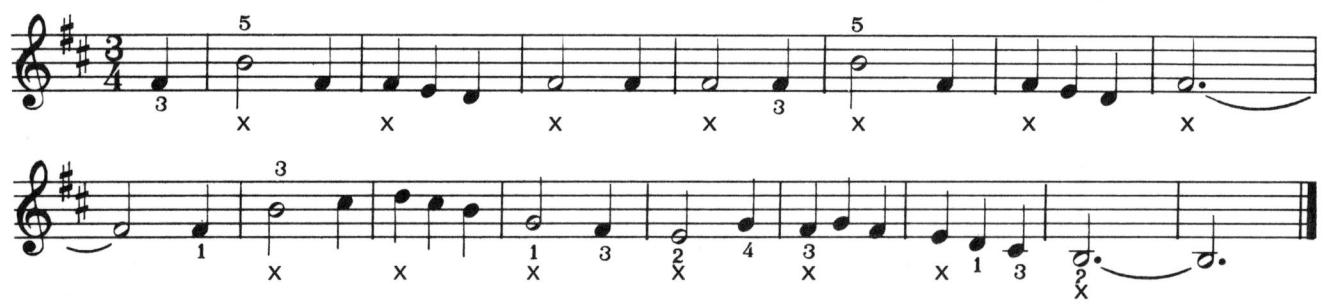

Italian Folk Song

Hungarian Folk Song

Le Chevalier

FRENCH FOLK SONG

59

La Mere Michel

FRENCH

Irish Folk Song

Legende De St. Nicholas

FRENCH

CADENCES: SECOND SET

Position of the 5th:

Say: cm   fm   cm $\frac{6}{4}$ G$_7$ cm

Write and play in the following keys ($\downarrow$=72).

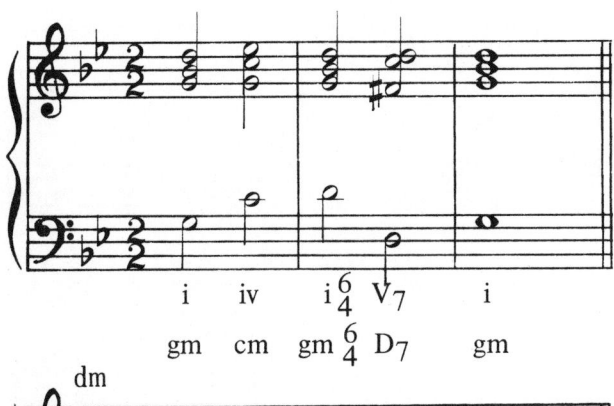

i   iv   i$\frac{6}{4}$ V$_7$ i

gm   cm   gm $\frac{6}{4}$ D$_7$ gm

i   iv   i$\frac{6}{4}$ V$_7$ i

fm   b$\flat$m   fm $\frac{6}{4}$ C$_7$ fm

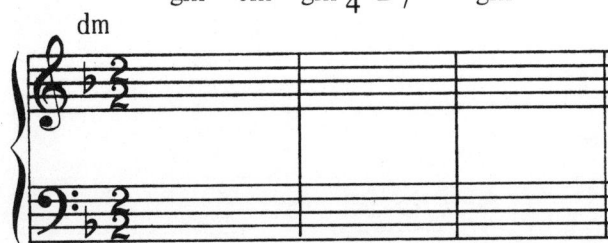

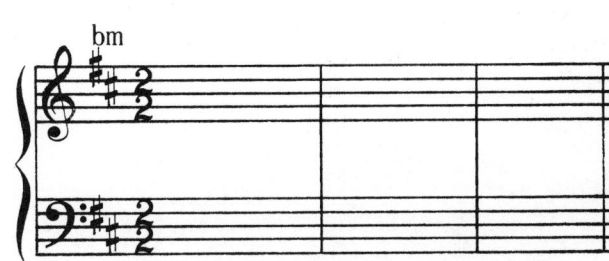

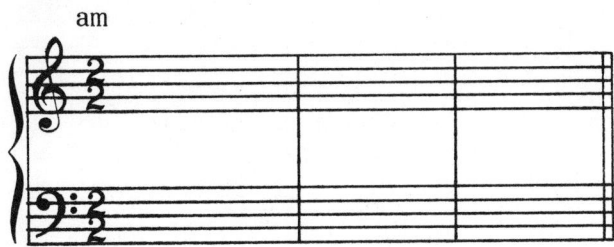

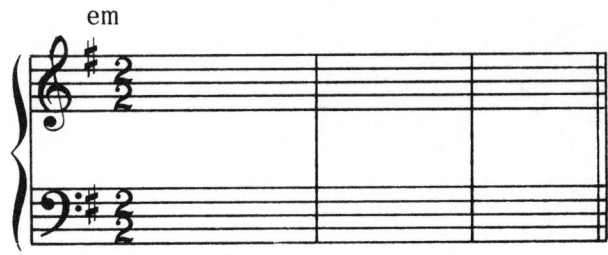

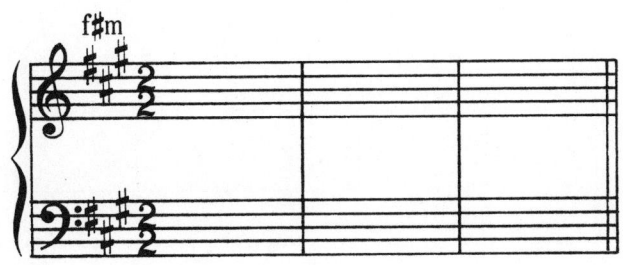

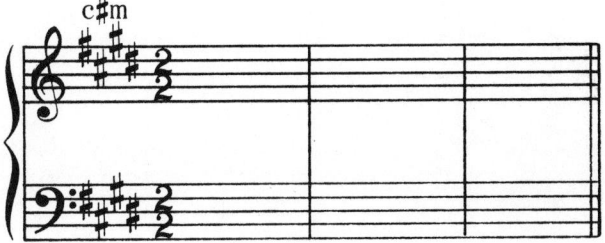

61

Position of the 8ve:

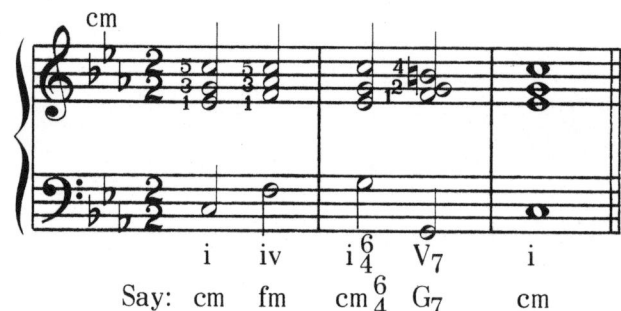

i   iv   i$^6_4$ V$_7$ i

Say: cm   fm   cm$^6_4$ G$_7$ cm

Write and play in the following keys ($\circ$ = 72).

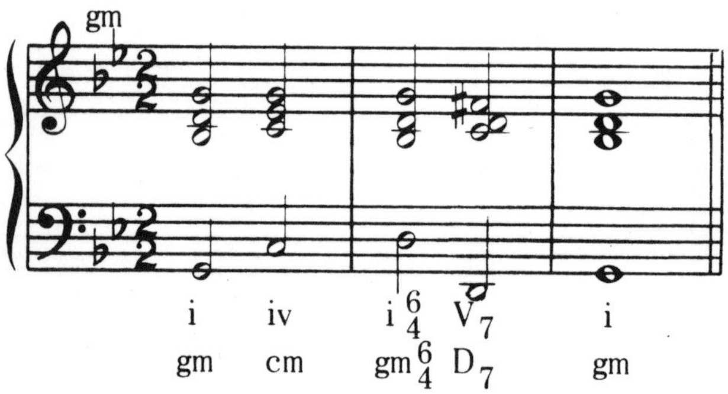

gm

i   iv   i$^6_4$ V$_7$ i

gm   cm   gm$^6_4$ D$_7$ gm

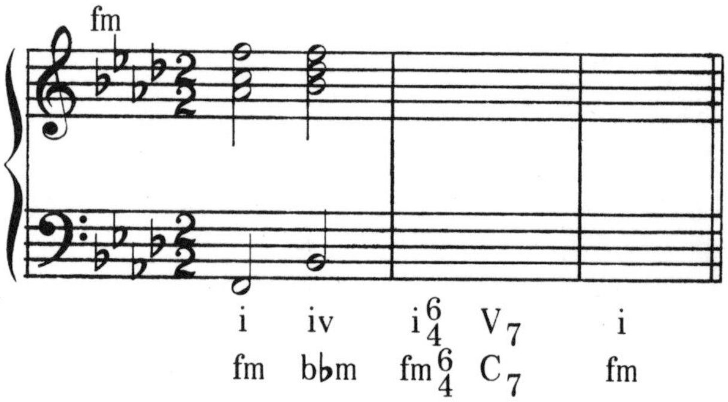

fm

i   iv   i$^6_4$ V$_7$ i

fm   b♭m   fm$^6_4$ C$_7$ fm

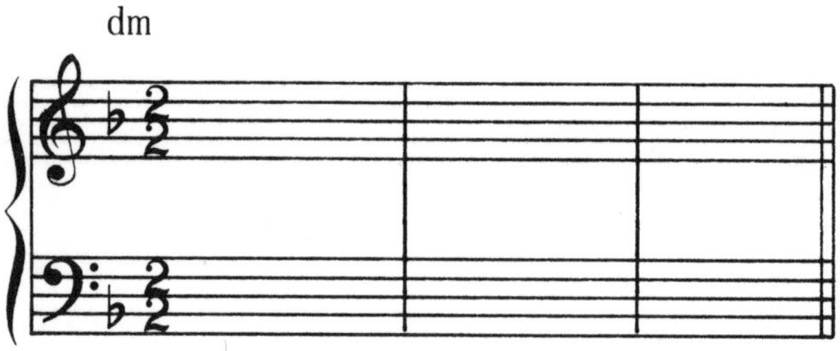

dm

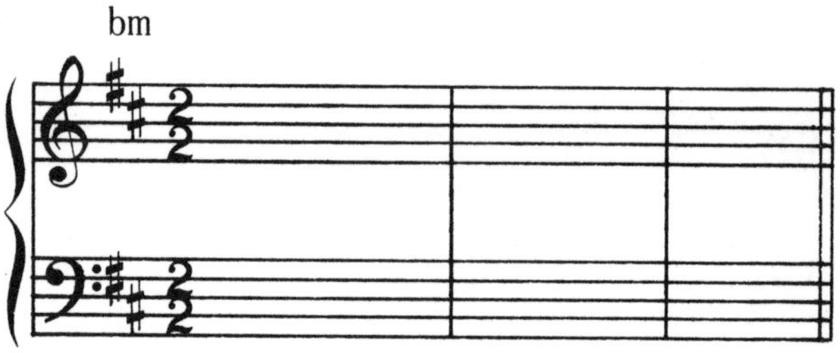

bm

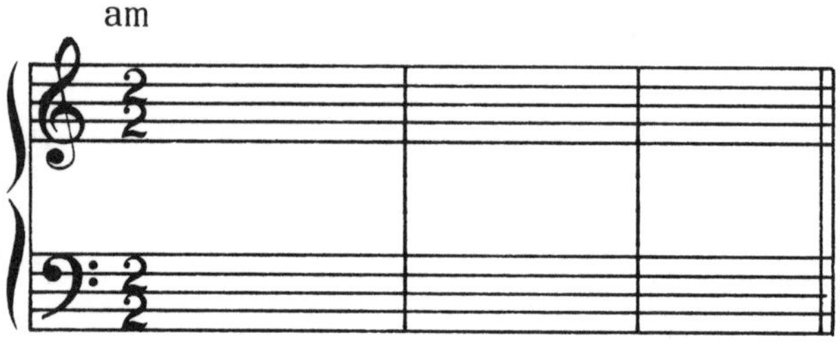

am

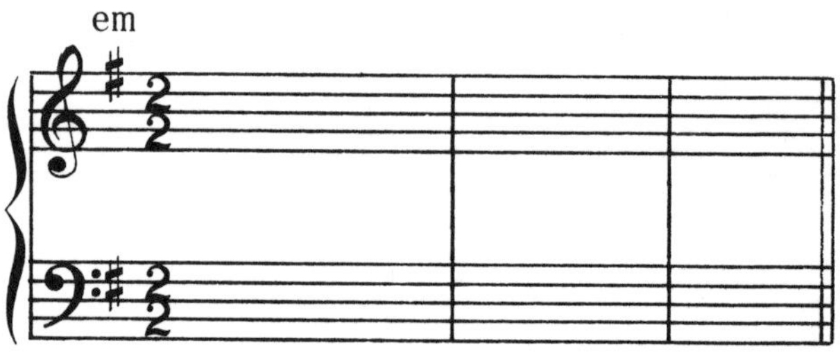

em

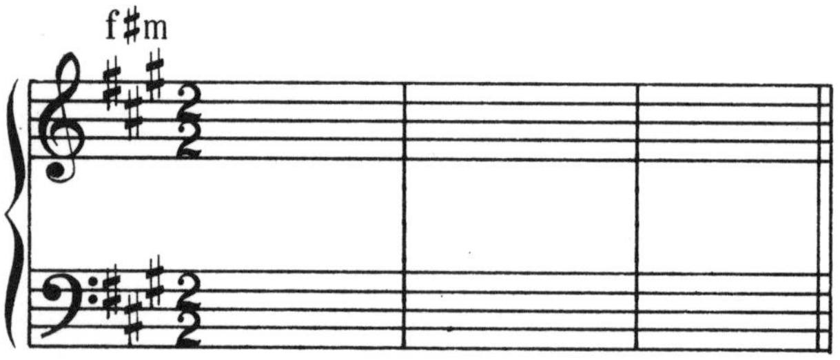

f♯m

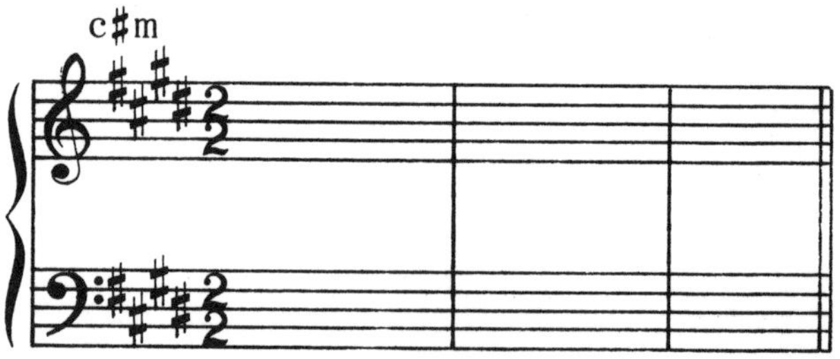

c♯m

Position of the 3rd:

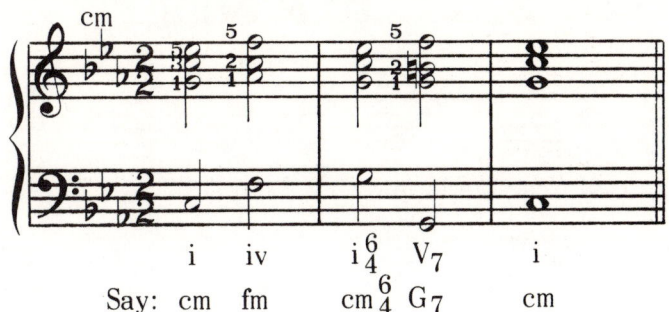

i   iv   i$_4^6$ V$_7$ i

Say: cm   fm   cm$_4^6$ G$_7$ cm

Write and play in the following keys ($\frac{}{}$ = 72).

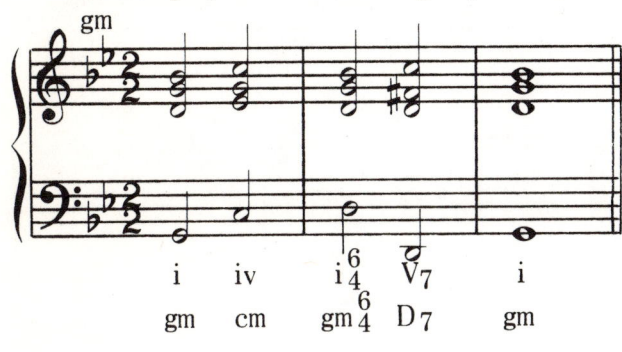

i   iv   i$_4^6$ V$_7$ i

gm   cm   gm$_4^6$ D$_7$ gm

i   iv   i$_4^6$ V$_7$ i

fm   b♭m   fm$_4^6$ C$_7$ fm

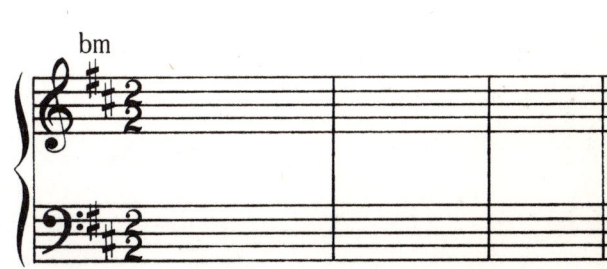

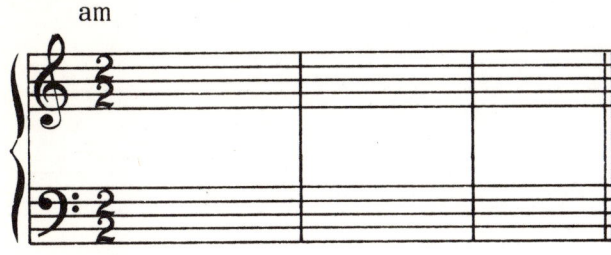

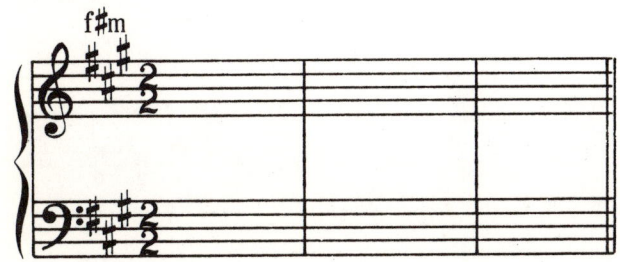

63

Syrian Folk Song

Play with left hand interval bass. Transpose to keys of fm, am.

Wayfaring Stranger
(Dorian)

i   IV$_4^6$ V^6 i

Say: dm   G$_4^6$ A^6 dm

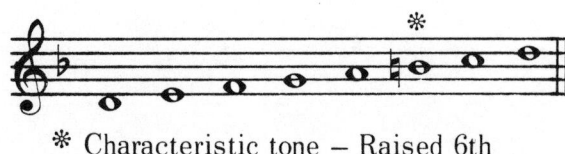

✻ Characteristic tone – Raised 6th

(Chords indicated by x):

Slow

FOLK BALLAD

Flowery Vale
(Dorian)

Chord Drill:

dm   am   dm   G   dm

Moderate

IRISH

Market Day
(Dorian)

Chord Drill:

dm   am   dm⁷   G   dm   dm

Fast   IRISH

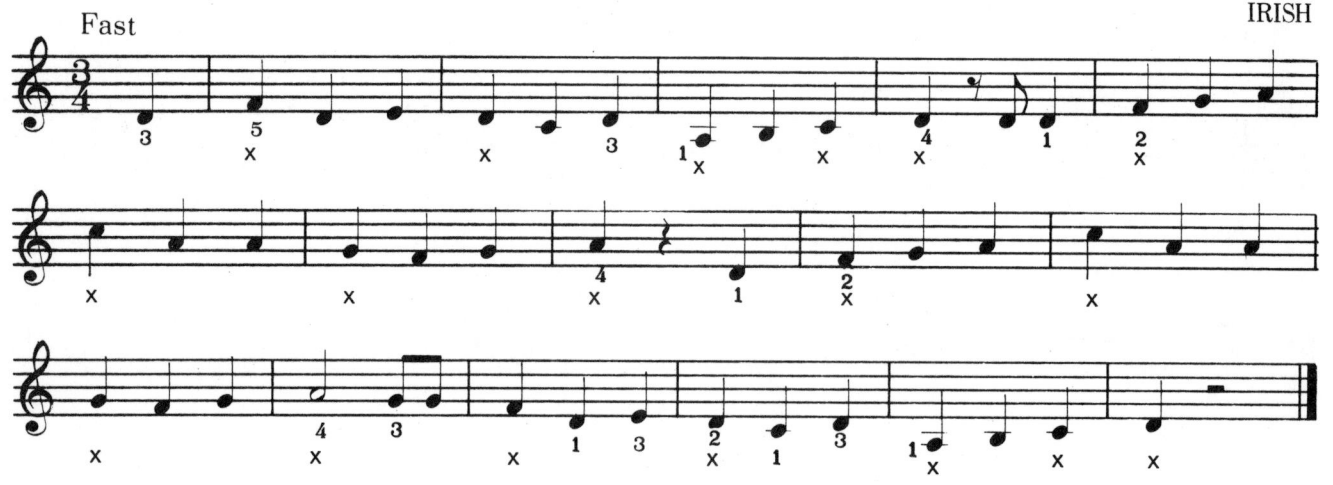

The Rosary
(Phrygian)

Chord Drill:

Slow   BRITTANY

66

Three Traitors
(Hypo—Lydian)*

Chord Drill:

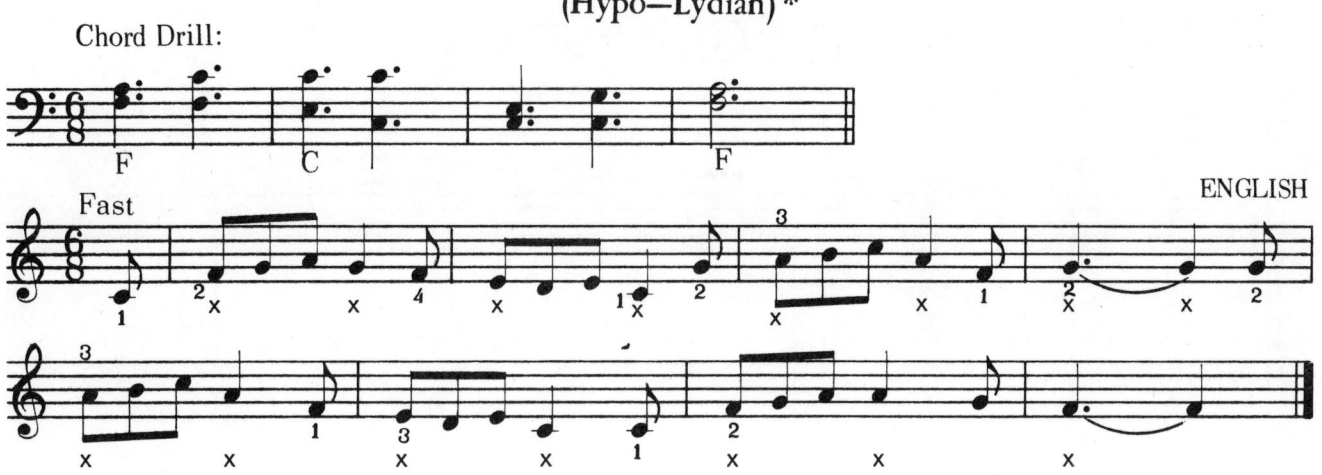

ENGLISH

The Crabfish
(Mixolydian)

Chord Drill:

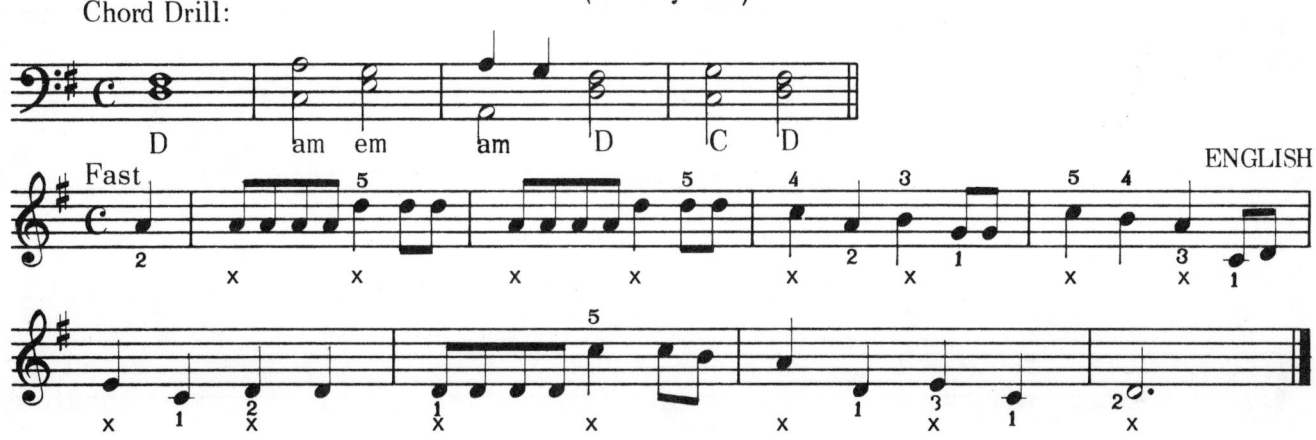

ENGLISH

Breton Canticle
(Aeolian)

Chord Drill:

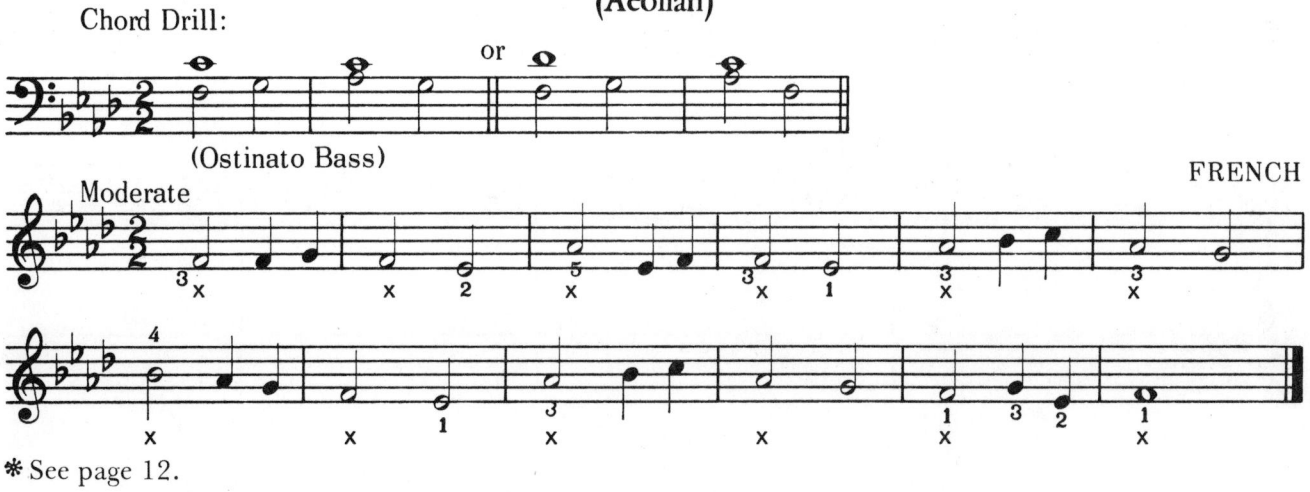

(Ostinato Bass)

FRENCH

Moderate

* See page 12.

The Glendy Burke

Complete the following bass part.

STEPHEN C. FOSTER 1826–1864

Polly Wolly Doodle

AMERICAN FOLK SONG

Play with left hand bouncing bass. Transpose to the key of F.

Buffalo Gals

Play with bouncing bass.

AMERICAN FOLK SONG

Camptown Races

Chord drill, bouncing bass:

STEPHEN C. FOSTER (1826-1864)

Home on the Range

Complete the Bass Part:

AMERICAN FOLK SONG

Home on the Range — (continued)

Refrain

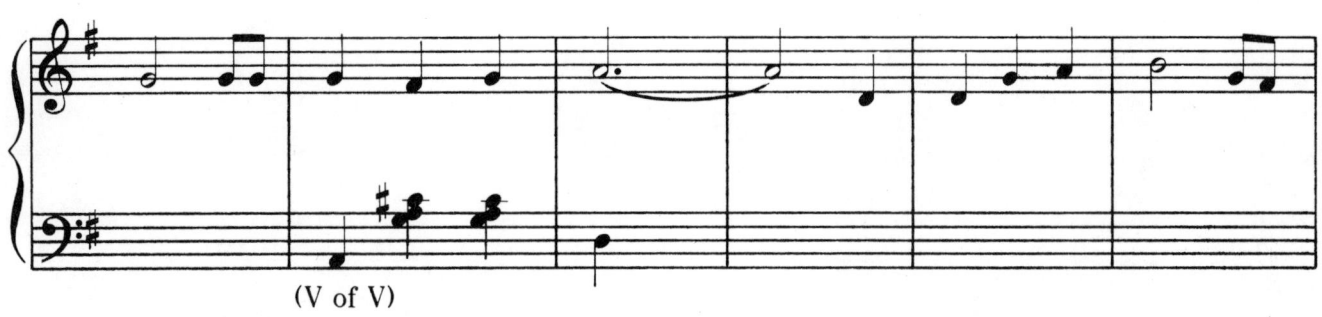

(V of V)

The Muffin Man

FOLK SONG

Old Woman

FOLK SONG

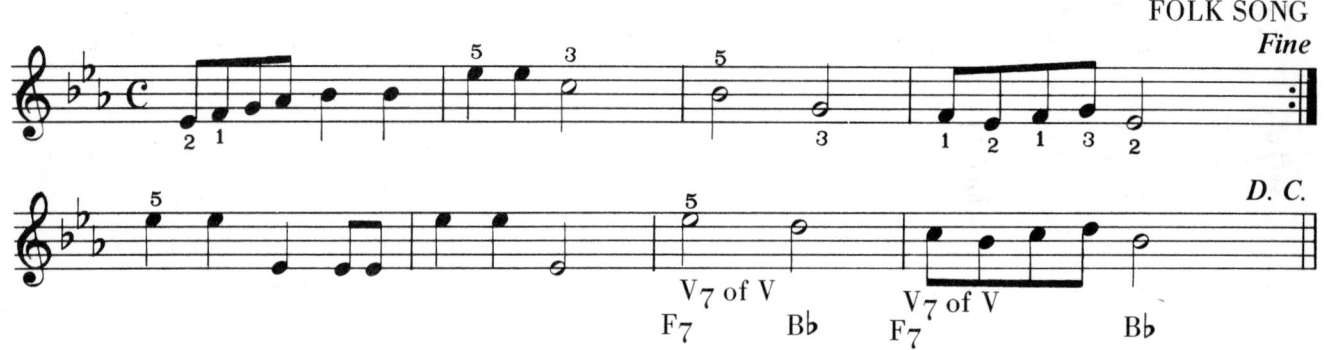

Holla Hi

GERMAN

Jingle Bells

PIERPONT

AMERICAN FOLK SONG

Over the River

Peer Nilson

DANISH

Little Pieces
in the Modes

Dorian

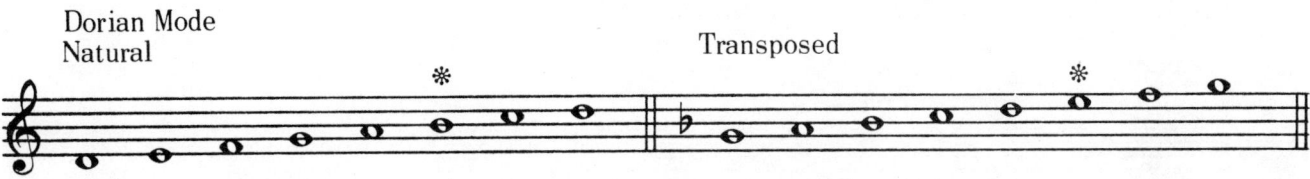

Dorian Mode
Natural

Transposed

❋ **Characteristic Tone**

Cheerfully

DOROTHY PRIESING

❋ cresc.

❋ Write your own fingering for this line.

Melody
(Ionian)

Moderato

DMITRI KABALEVSKY (1904–)

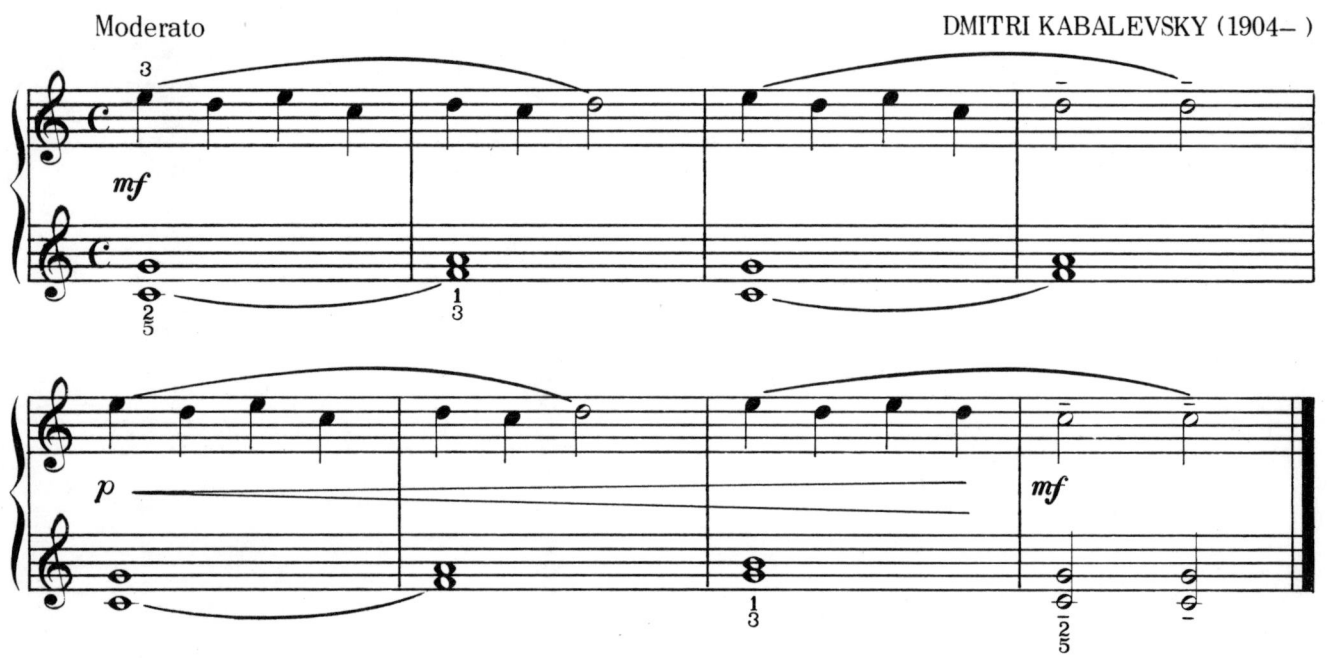

Rambling
(Aeolian)

Moderato

DMITRI KABALEVSKY (1904–)

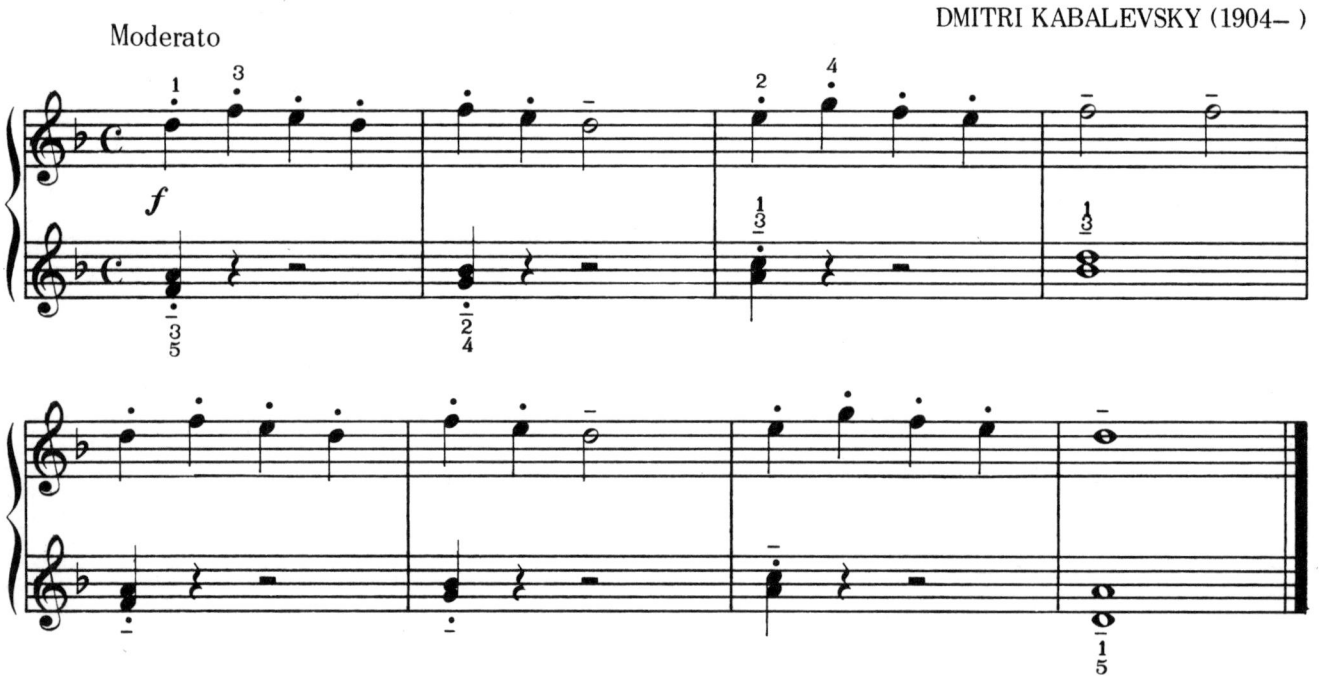

Song
(Dorian)

Andante

DMITRI KABALEVSKY (1904–)

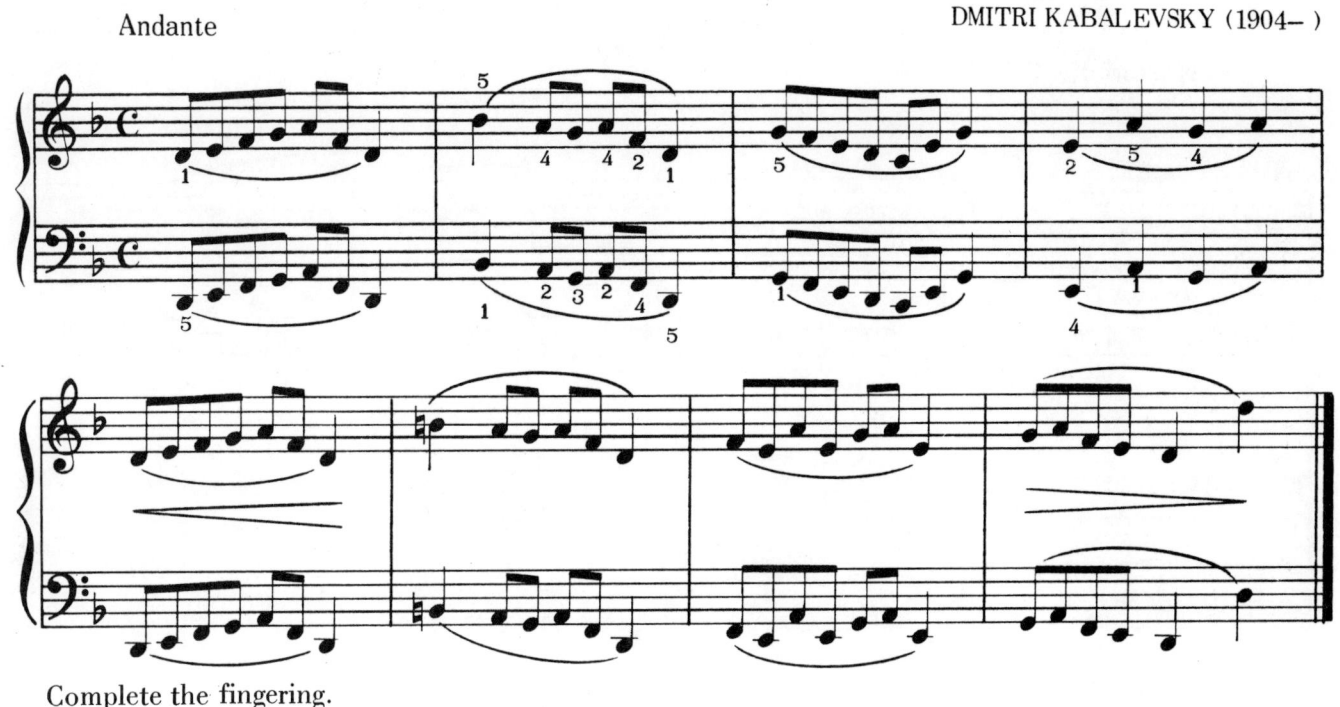

Complete the fingering.

A Little Dance
(Ionian)

Allegro molto

DMITRI KABALEVSKY (1904–)

79

Phrygian

Phrygian Mode
Natural

Transposed

* Characteristic Tone

Sadly

DOROTHY PRIESING

Lydian

Lydian
Natural

Transposed

* Characteristic Tone

Fast

DOROTHY PRIESING

*Complete the fingering.

The Drunken Sailor

(Dorian)

Arr. by D.M.P.

❋ Characteristic tone

Mixolydian

Mixolydian
Natural

Transposed

✻ Characteristic Tone

Spirited

DOROTHY PRIESING

Mazurka

(Phrygian)

DOROTHY PRIESING

❋ Characteristic tone

Lilliput March

(Lydian)

HUNGARY
Arr. by D.M.P.

✻ Characteristic tone

Aeolian

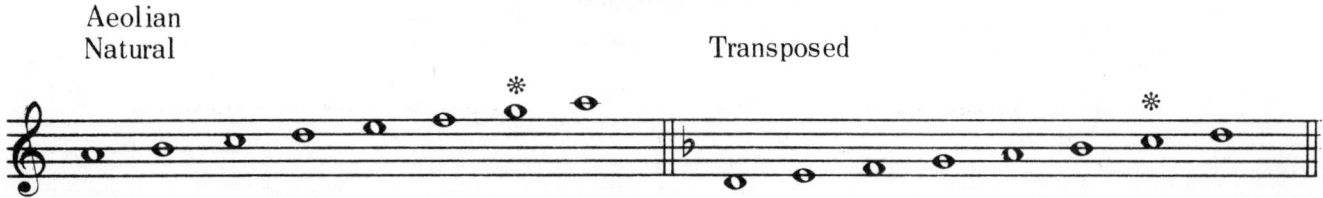

Aeolian
Natural

Transposed

❋ Characteristic Tone

Slow

DOROTHY PRIESING

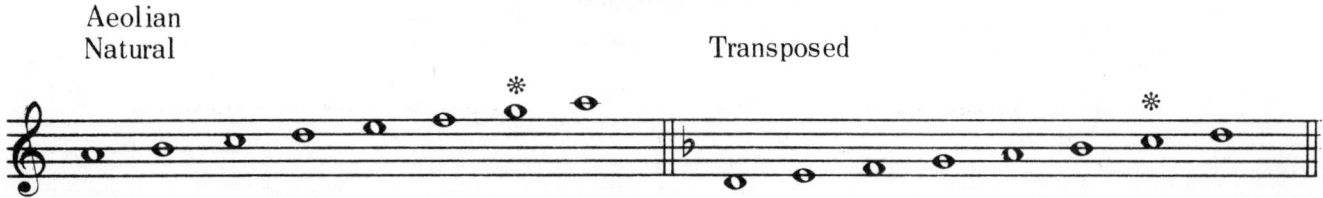

Fanfare

(After Thomas Weelkes)

(Mixolydian)

DOROTHY PRIESING

Characteristic tone

What adaptations have to be made in dividing parts between the hands?

Aeolian Dance

(Aeolian)

Moderato

DOROTHY PRIESING

* Characteristic tone

When Jesus Wept

(Aeolian)

WILLIAM BILLINGS (1746-1800)
Arr. by D.M.P.

※ Characteristic tone

Locate the melody in each phrase. Is it always in the soprano?

High Barbary

(Aeolian)

ENGLISH
Arr. by D.M.P.

✻ Characteristic tone

Reuben, Reuben

(A Study in Whole-Tone Scale)

Moderato

SALVATORE LAGATTUTA

Flowery Vale

(Pentatonic)

IRISH
Arr. by D.M.P.

What compositional technic do you see here?

TO PINNOCHIO

March

RUSSELL HAYTON

Mazurka

(Phrygian)

F. CHOPIN (1810-1849)
Op. 41, No. 1

✻ Characteristic tone

THEME FROM # Symphony #4—Second Movement

(Phrygian)

J. BRAHMS (1833-1897)

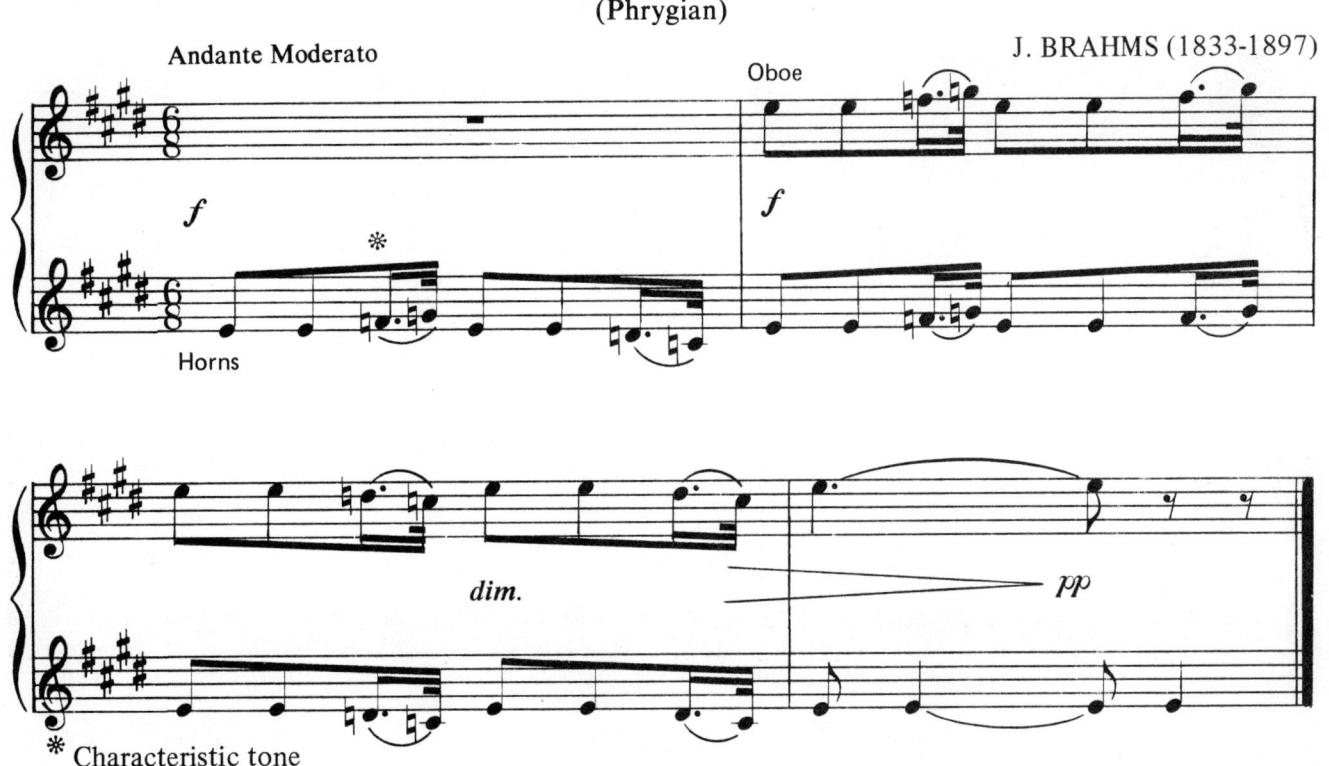

✻ Characteristic tone

Community Songs

THREE VERSIONS OF
America

HENRY CAREY (1687–1743)
Arr. by AHZ

A. First Version

Play also in key of F.

America

B. Choral Style

HENRY CAREY (1687–1743)

Recite chord names as you play. Memorize the chord structure.
Transpose to the key of F.

pt = passing tone
o 7 = diminished seventh

98

America

HENRY CAREY (1687–1743)

C. Full Chord Style (for Community Sing Accompaniment)

Complete the analysis.

I   vi   ii⁶   V   -   -   etc.

Say: F   dm   gm⁶   C   -   -

pt = passing tone

THREE VERSIONS OF
The Star-Spangled Banner

JOHN STAFFORD SMITH
Arr. by AHZ

A. First Version

The Star-Spangled Banner (continued)

The Star-Spangled Banner

B. Choral Style

JOHN STAFFORD SMITH
Arr. by AHZ

ln = lower neighbor
Recite chord names as you play.

The Star-Spangled Banner (continued)

Double thirds

V^7
Eb^7

ln

I	V^6_4	I^6	V	V^4_2	I^6	vi	V of V	V
Ab	Eb^6_4	Ab^6	Eb	Eb^4_2	Ab^6	fm	Bb^7	Eb

pt   pt   S
pt   pt

I	I^6	IV	V of ii	ii	ii^6 vii $ø7$	$^6_4$	V	$^4_2$
A	Ab^6	Db	F^4_3	bbm	bbm^6 $dø7$	Ab^6_4	Eb	$^4_2$

pt   et

I^6	V	I	I^6	vi	ii^4_3	I^6_4	V^7	I
Ab^6	Eb	Ab	Ab^6	fm	Bb^4_3	Ab^6_4	Eb^7	Ab

S = Suspension
o7 = diminished seventh
et = escape tone

103

The Star-Spangled Banner

C. Full Chord Version

JOHN STAFFORD SMITH
Arr. by AHZ

The Star-Spangled Banner (continued)

TWO VERSIONS OF
America, the Beautiful

A. First Version

SAMUEL A. WARD (1847–1903)

Arr. by AHZ

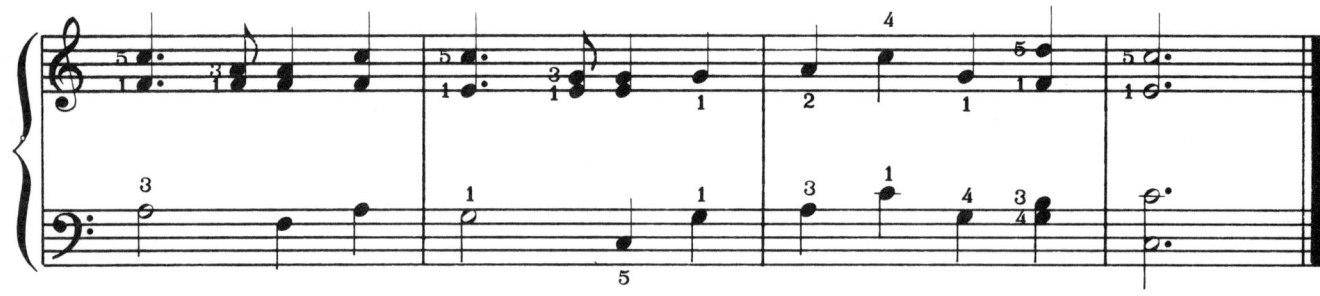

America, the Beautiful

B. Chorale Style (for community singing)

SAMUEL A. WARD (1847–1903)

* Note melody in bass
S = Suspension
ln = lower neighbor
pt = passing tone
o7 = diminished seventh

Music Reading

Sight-reading

Good sight-reading skill depends on:
1. Observations before playing:
   a. Key signature.
   b. Meter signature.
   c. Tempo markings.
   d. Recognition of like and unlike phrases.
2. Setting a tempo suited to the stage of advancement: set a tempo slow enough to permit complete coordination between eye, brain and fingers. "Halting" playing will not produce a good sight-reader. Speed comes after coordination has been established.
3. Keeping your eyes on the score. (It may be helpful to cover the keys.)
4. Locating the keys by touch. (Play blind.)
5. Identifying special features of the score such as chord structure, rhythmic groups, etc.
6. Reading horizontally, not vertically. A chord does not mean anything by itself. Its progression is important. Be aware of the chord's progression to the next beat and to the end of the phrase.
7. If the arrangements in this section seem too difficult for one player, they may be played as duos or trios by several players. Be sure to keep the tempo steady.

Game Song

Unison and block chords:

GERMAN FOLK SONG
Arr. by R.H.

Transpose to the key of F.

Caterpillar!

Analyze for like and unlike phrases.
Note chromatic figures.
May be played by multiple players (Soprano, Bass).

RUSSIAN FOLK SONG
Arr. by R.H.

113

Who Are You?

Note: Syncopated accompaniment.
Melody is an exact repetition of period with different harmonization.
Analyze the differences in harmonization.
Write your own fingering.

GERMAN FOLK SONG
Arr. by R.H.

Autumn

Analyze for like and contrasting phrases.
Note thirds and mixed rhythms.
May be played by multiple players.

BOHEMIAN FOLK SONG
Arr. by R.H.

Winter Night

Note: Syncopation in accompaniment.

SLAVONIC FOLK SONG
Arr. by R.H.

Winter's Past

Note: Broken chords.
Melody is an exact repetition of period with different harmonization.
Analyze the differences. Imitation of right and left hand parts.

GERMAN FOLK SONG
Arr. by R.H.

Vigiles Et Sancti

May be played by multiple players.
Boldly

COLOGNE GESANGBUCH, 1623
Arr. by R.H.

A Song of Ships

Analyze for like and unlike phrases.
Note dotted notes and characteristic rhythms.
May be played by multiple players.

ENGLISH FOLK SONG
Arr. by R.H.

119

Minuet IV

(From Anna Magdalena Book)

J. S. BACH (1685–1750)

Minuet IV (continued)

The Good Adventure

May be performed by two or three players, one to a part.
Analyze for like and unlike phrases.
Note use of thirds and sixths.

FRENCH FOLK SONG
Arr. by R.H.

Lullaby

OLD SONG
Arr. by R.H.

Note: The piece consists of an exact repeated period as far as the melody is concerned with the melody and exact accompaniment measures being interchanged from the right to left hand.

Old French Song

Note: Structure of like and unlike phrases.
Write a fingering for this piece.

Arr. by R.H.

The Letter Box

Note the imitation of the two parts.

GERMAN FOLK SONG
Arr. by R.H.

Dutch Song

Analyze for like and contrasting phrases.
Note: The bass is the melody inverted.
May be played by multiple players dividing the parts.

FOLK SONG
Arr. by R.H.

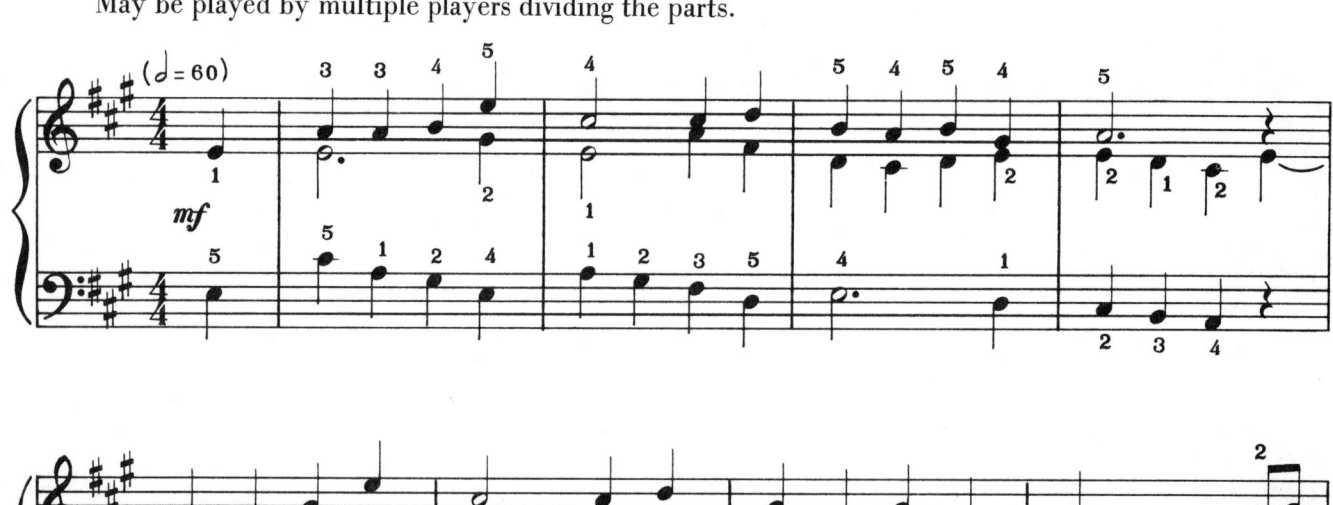

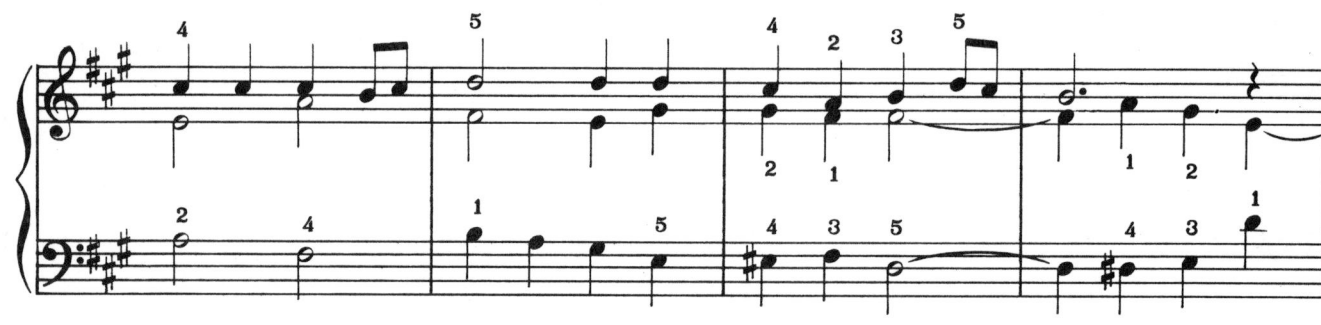

The Flag

Note: The octave bass.
Play with chords struck precisely together.

GERMAN FOLK SONG
Arr. by R.H.

* More advanced players may play octaves.

The Use of the Pedals

The piano has three pedals. The one on the extreme right is the damper pedal, so named because it raises *all* the dampers from the strings, allowing the tones struck to be sustained and broadened by sympathetic vibration. The one in the middle is called the sostenuto pedal. It holds the dampers on *only those strings* struck at the moment (until the sostenuto is released), thus permitting the sustaining of a single chord or tone while other harmonies or notes are played elsewhere on the keyboard. The pedal on the left is known as the "soft pedal."

Use of the Damper Pedal: The most common pedaling is called syncopated pedal; the effect is that of smoothing, enriching or binding together tones sounded while the pedal is held down. Play the scale of triads in the key of C. Pedal after each chord, releasing as you play the next chord. As you play, say "up" on the chord, "down" between chords, as follows:

Now play the chord progression twice as fast (half notes). Continue pedaling as before. Finally, try the exercise in quarter notes and in broken chords. The *rule for damper pedaling* is to change the pedal immediately after the chord change. Avoid pedal on scale passages: listen for blurring.

Use of the Sostenuto Pedal: A real sostenuto pedal is usually found only on grand pianos. A single chord to be sustained (usually in the bass register) is struck, the sostenuto pressed and held while other notes are played.

Use of the Soft Pedal: This is used only when *una corda* (one string) is printed in the score. On grand pianos the action shifts upward (to the right) so that the hammers strike one instead of three strings, resulting in a much thinner, softer tone.

Other Types of pedaling are used in more advanced piano playing, always subject to approval by the critical ear.

Pedal Marking: Pedaling is marked under the score as is indicated in the example above (*Ped.**). The pedal pressed on "*Ped.*" and released on *. At times, also it is marked as follows:

Down   Release

A number of previous selections would sound good with pedaling.

Waltz

Note: Similar and contrasting phrases.
      Last phrase is like first and second phrases but embellished with variation devices.
      Chromatic texture of last two phrases.
      Use damper pedal.
      Suggestion: Play the accompaniment part with two hands while the class sings melody.

GERMAN FOLK SONG
Arr. by R.H.

The Swing

Note: Like and contrasting phrases.
Use damper pedal. |_____|
Play the accompaniment part with both hands while the class sings the melody.

GERMAN FOLK SONG
Arr. by R.H.

Transpose to the key of F.

Au Clair de la Lune

May be played by multiple players.
Note: Like and contrasting phrases.
         Use of different tonal texture to harmonize like phrases.
         Use of sixths in texture.
         Use damper pedal.

FRENCH FOLK SONG
Arr. by R.H.

No pedal

with pedal

We Plow the Fields

May be played by multiple players.
Note the rhythmic harmonic structure as marked
in the first seven measures. Complete marking.

JOHANN SCHULTZ (1800)
Arr. by RH

Refrain

Austria

May be played with multiple players.
With majesty

FRANZ JOSEPH HAYDN (1797)
Arr. by RH

Adeste Fidelis

May be played by multiple players.
With joyful dignity

I. F. WADE'S CANTUS DIVERSI (1751)
Arr. by RH

Sicilian Mariners Hymn

May be played by multiple players.

SICILIAN MELODY, pun. 1794
Arr. by RH

Chorale and Open Score Reading

The functional pianist is frequently called on to play four-part chordal types of music such as church hymns and chorales. Good playing in this idiom demands:

1. Firm touch.
2. Strict rhythm.
3. Care to give every measure its total amount of time.
4. Exactness of dotted rhythms.
5. Precision in playing left and right-hand parts simultaneously. (Many pianists develop the bad habit, in playing chordal style, of playing the left hand slightly ahead of the right. This is to be avoided.)

The following pages are designed to develop the techniques you will need to acquire this skill.

1. Analyze (and write analysis under each of the following chants).
2. Set a tempo suitable to your present stage of advancement.
3. Play with precision.

The chants offer an excellent opportunity for the student to acquire pedaling technique.

Chants

Write your own fingering.

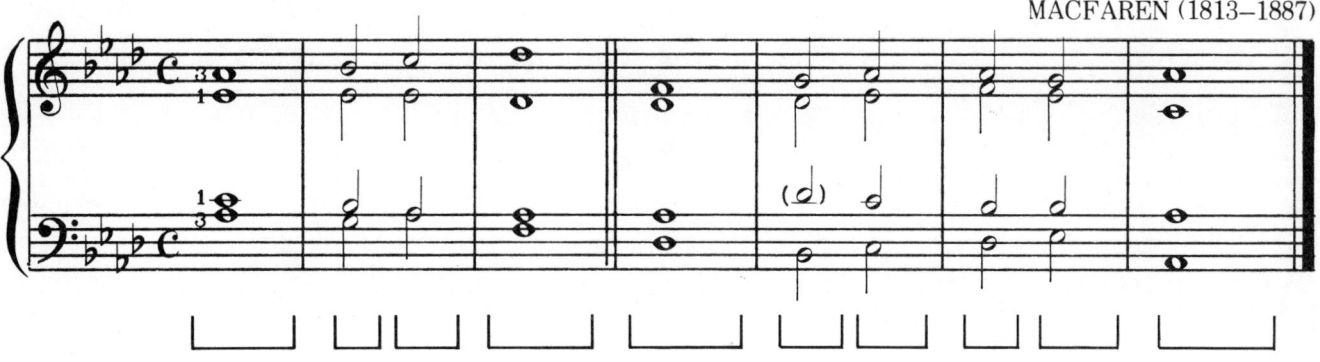

Continue pedaling as above.

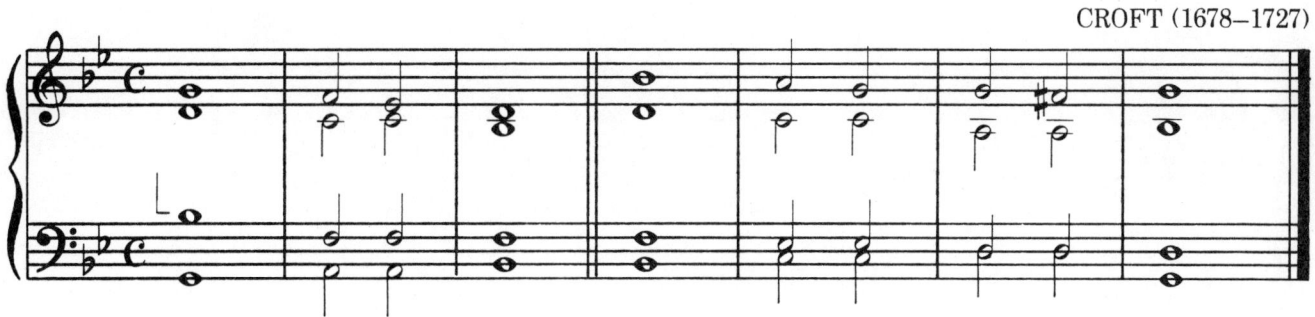

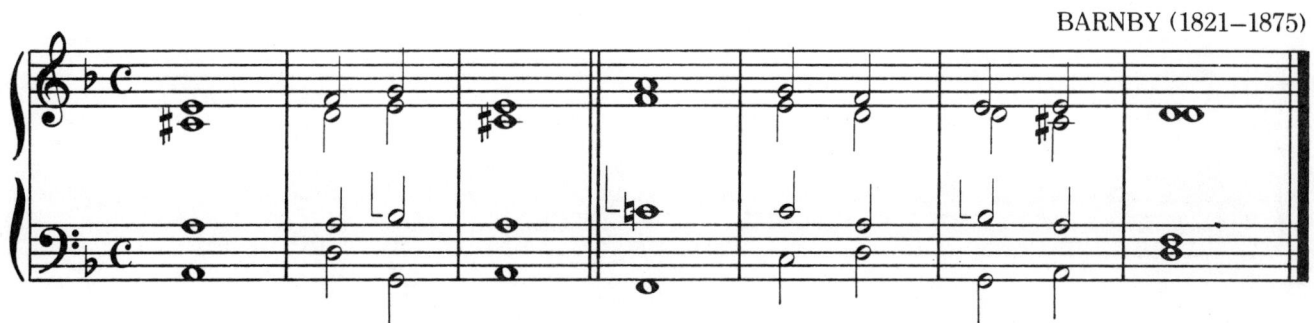

Chants (continued)

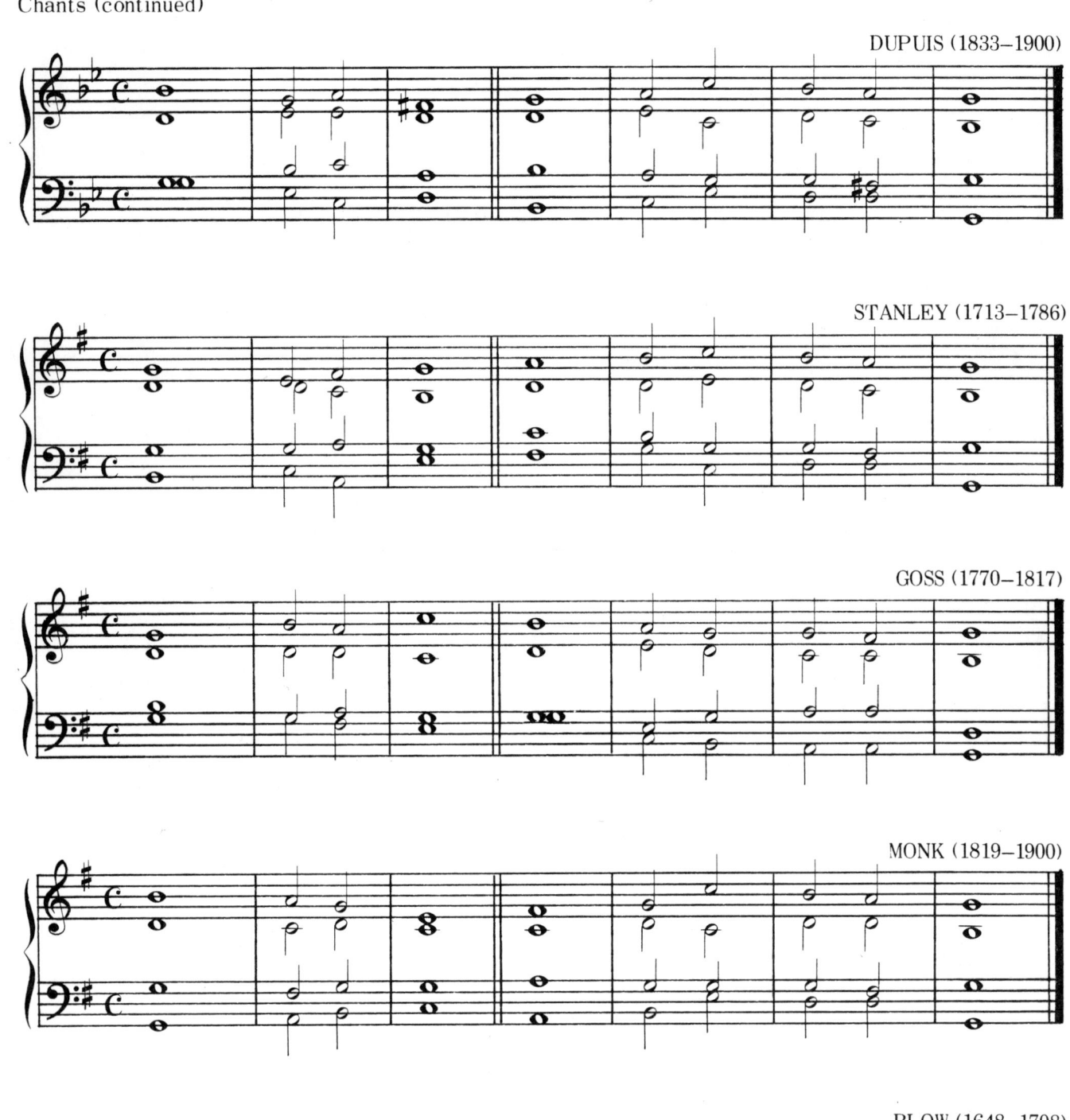

DUPUIS (1833–1900)

STANLEY (1713–1786)

GOSS (1770–1817)

MONK (1819–1900)

BLOW (1648–1708)

Having mastered the chants, practice the following until they can be played at proper tempo with surety.

The printed page of music appears in several forms and the functional pianist must become familiar and proficient in all styles. Frequently, choral music will be printed with the stems to indicate the part leading. For example, all soprano note stems will be up and all alto note stems down on the treble staff. Some of the following are printed in this fashion.

O God, Our Help in Ages Past

WILLIAM CROFT (1678–1727)

Blest Be the Tie That Binds

HANS G. NAGELI (1773–1836)

Blest Be the Tie That Binds (continued)

Now Thank We All Our God

The fermata (⌢) in music of the period of Johann Cruger means a breath and not a hold.

JOHANN CRUGER (1598–1662)

140

Cast Thy Burden upon the Lord

FELIX MENDELSSOHN (1809–1847)

141

God Reveals His Presence

NEANDER (1680)

O Morning Star

PHILLIP NIKOLAI (1599)

Since Now the Day Hath Reached Its Close

DARMSTADT HYMN BOOK (1698)

Now God Be with Us

FRIEDRICH F. FLEMMING (1778–1813)

Praise God, from Whom All Blessings Flow

LOUIS BOUREGEOIS (1510–?)

Now the Day Is Over

JOSEPH BARNBY (1838–1896)

The Ash Grove

WELSH FOLK SONG

Four-Part Open Score

Playing parts for choral rehearsal involves reading an open score. Some excerpts from choral literature follow:

It is suggested that the student, according to his ability

1. Read and play the soprano and alto together.
2. Read and play the tenor and bass together.
3. Read and play the soprano and bass together.
4. Read and play the alto and tenor together.
5. Read and play all four parts together.

From Ill Do Thou Defend Us

J. S. BACH (1685–1750)

EXCERPT FROM
Et in terra pax hominibus
from the "Gloria"

ANTONIO VIVALDI (1675–1743)

148

EXCERPT FROM

My Soul, Now Bless Thy Maker

J. S. BACH (1685—1750)

The student is urged to further his skill in open-score reading by using such other octavo editions of choral music as are available to him.

Selected Pieces

Three Pieces

I

(♩ = 120)

HASSLER (1747—1822)

153

II

HASSLER (1747–1822)

154

III

HASSLER (1747–1822)

155

Minuet V

(From Anna Magdalena Book)

J. S. BACH (1685–1750)

Minuet V (continued)

157

Minka

RUSSIAN FOLK SONG
Arr. by AHZ

Don Juan

W. A. MOZART (1756–1791)

Ed. by AHZ

159

Minuet XIV

(From the Anna Magdalena Book)

Note: canonical imitation.

J. S. BACH (1685–1750)

Minuetto

DOMENICO SCARLATTI (1659-1725)
Ed. by AHZ

Polonaise

(From the Anna Magdalena Book)

J. S. BACH (1685–1750)

Bouree

G. PHILLIP TELEMANN (1681–1767)

Ed. by AHZ

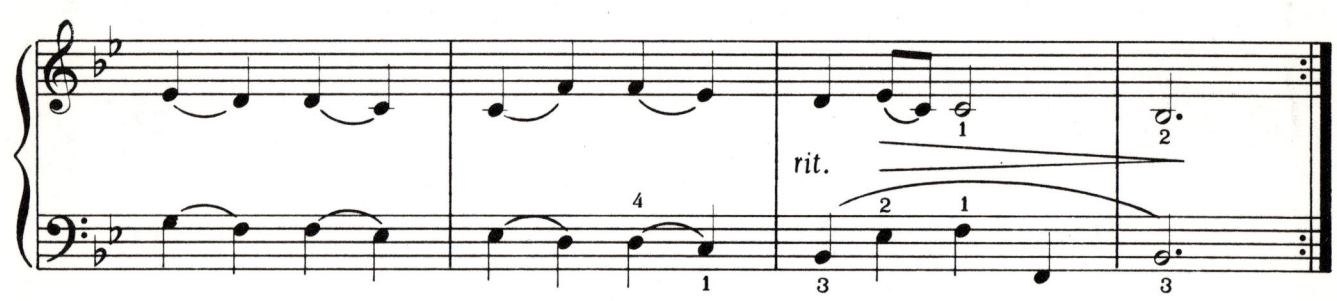

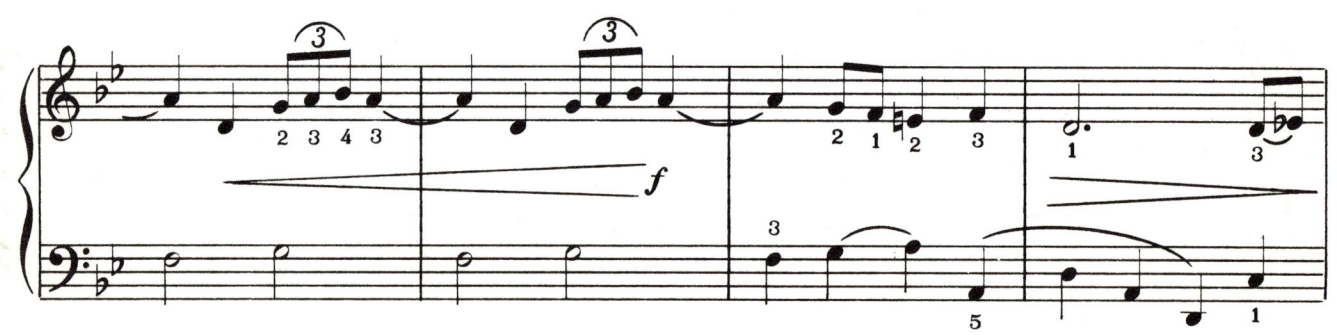

Bouree (continued)

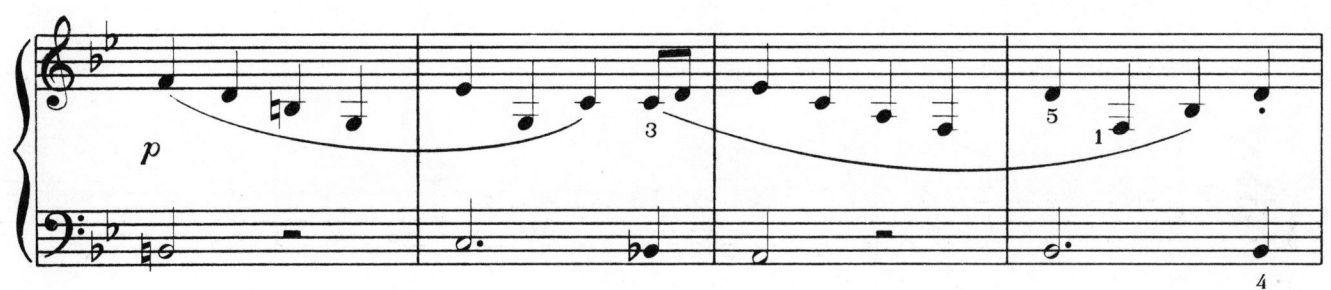

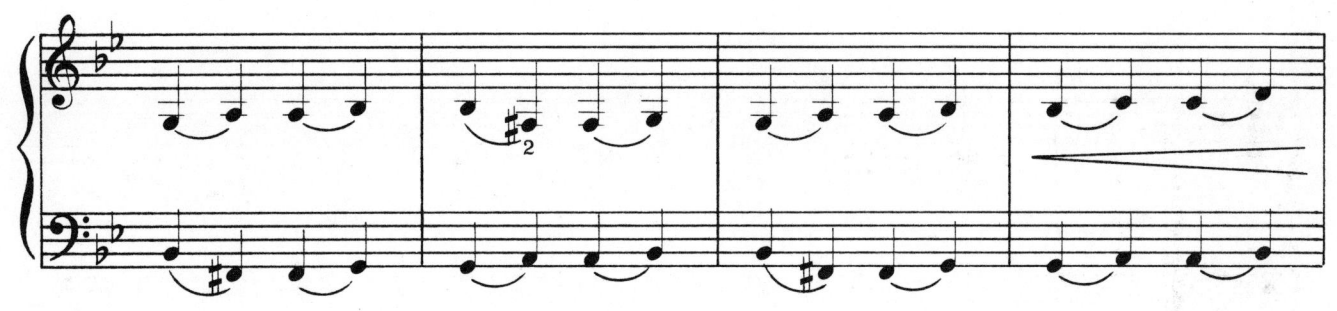

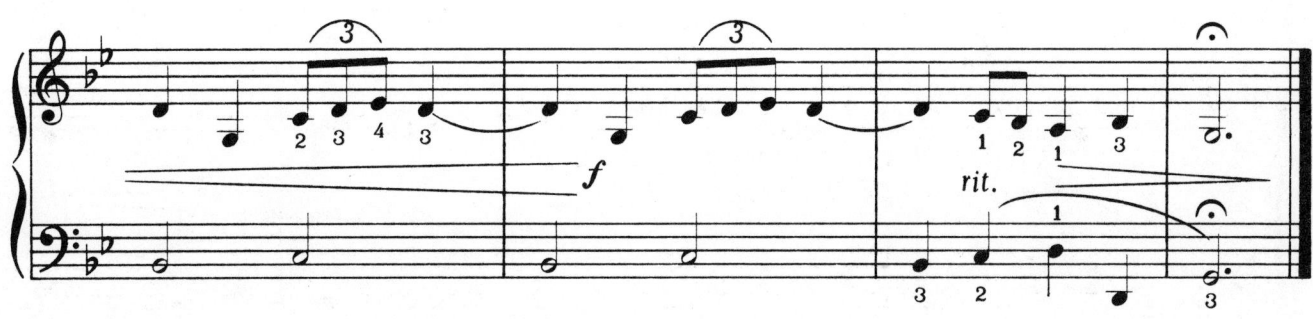

March from Lucia

GAETANO DONIZETTI (1797–1848)
Arr. by AHZ

Minuet

G. PHILLIP TELEMANN (1681–1767)
Ed. by AHZ

Andantino

JOSEPH HAYDN (1732–1809)
Ed. by AHZ

Andantino (continued)

169

Minuet

JOHANN BUTTSTEDT (1666–1727)
Ed. by AHZ

Andante

J. W. HASSLER (1747–1822)

Ed. by AHZ

Pastorale Dance

LUDWIG VAN BEETHOVEN (1779–1827)
Ed. by AHZ

Pastorale Dance (continued)

Allemande

LUDWIG VAN BEETHOVEN (1770–1827)
Ed. by AHZ

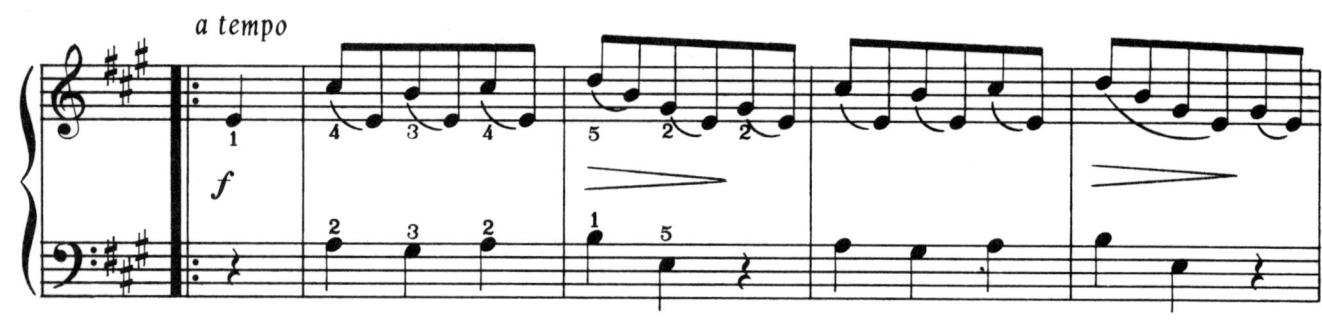

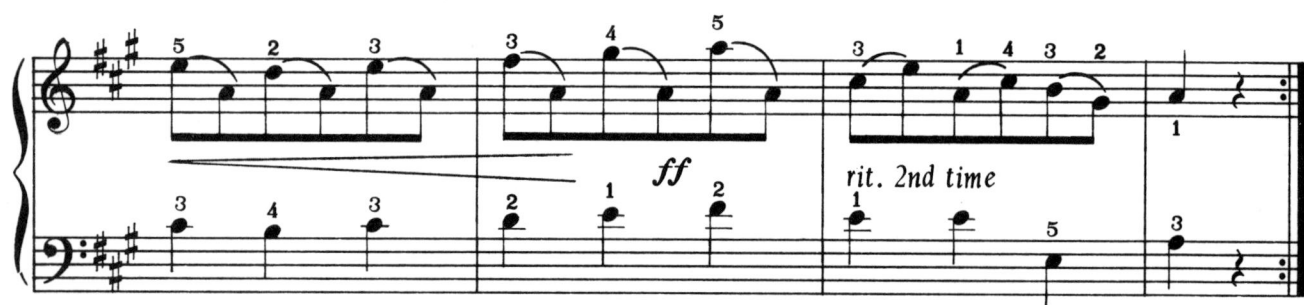

Burleske

L. MOZART (1719–1787)
Ed. by AHZ

Entree

L. MOZART (1719–1787)
Ed. by AHZ

175

Waltz

LUDWIG VAN BEETHOVEN (1770–1827)
Ed. by AHZ

Waltz (continued)

Waltz (continued)

Teasing

BARTOK (1881–1945)

179

Teasing (continued)

Round

BARTOK (1881–1945)

Andante

Dorian

DOROTHY PRIESING

Write your own fingering for this piece.
Flowing

Pentatonic Boogie

DOROTHY PRIESING

On Repetition of Part I more advanced players can alternate phrases 8va.

Black and White

(Pentatonic Melody under a Pedal Point)

RUSSELL HAYTON

Lento

Espressivo

Black and White (continued)

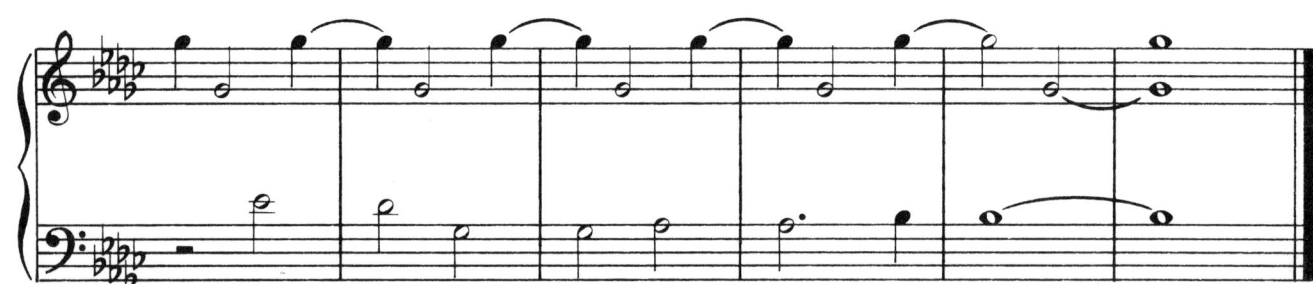

March

D. SHOSTAKOVICH (1906-1975)

Waltz

D. SHOSTAKOVICH (1906-1975)

Waltz

DMITRI KABALEVSKY (1904–)

Moderato

Clowns

DMITRI KABALEVSKY (1904–)

Allegro

Minuet VII

(From the Anna Magdalena Book)

J. S. BACH (1685–1750)

Minuet VII (continued)

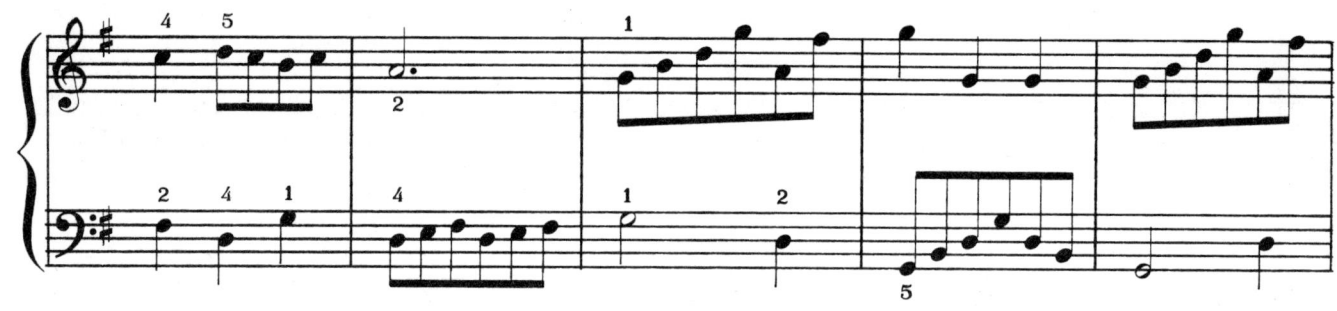

Musette

(From the Anna Magdalena Book)

J. S. BACH (1685–1750)

Galop

Animato

DMITRI KABALEVSKY (1904–)

Folk Dance

DMITRI KABALEVSKY (1904–)

Day Dream

Rhythm Study

RUSSELL HAYTON

Cherry Blossoms

RUSSELL HAYTON

Moderato (= 60)

*Pedal ——

p

rit.

* Hold the damper pedal down for the whole composition.

Soldier's March

Tempo di marcia

ROBERT SCHUMANN (1810-1856)

The Merry Farmer

Allegro Moderato

ROBERT SCHUMANN (1810-1856)

Peter and the Wolf

PROKOFIEV (1891–1953)
Arr. by AHZ

Peter's Theme

Carefree (♩ = 80)

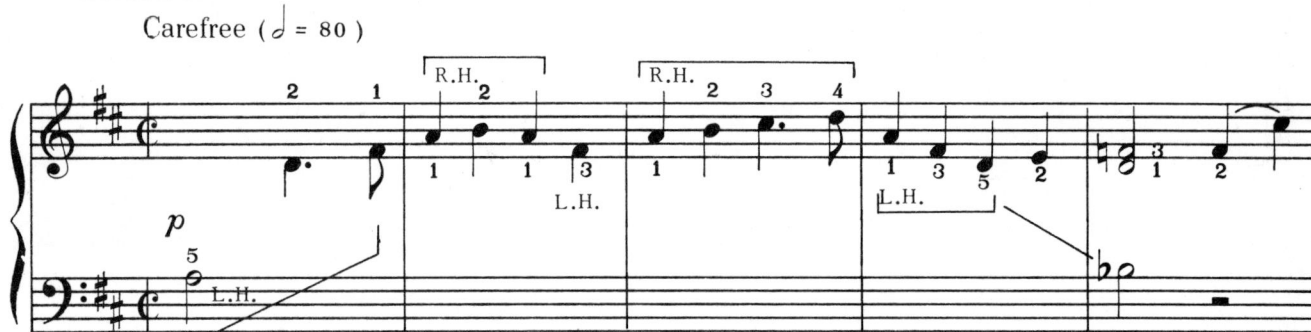

The Cat

Stealthily

Peter and the Wolf (continued)

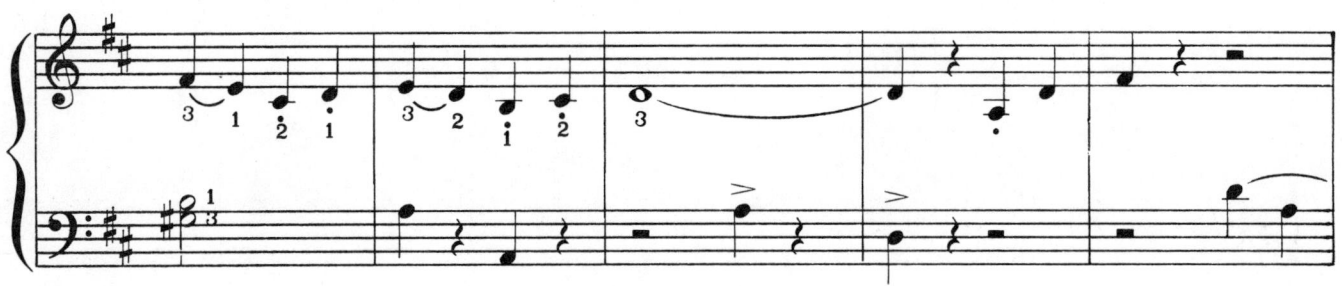

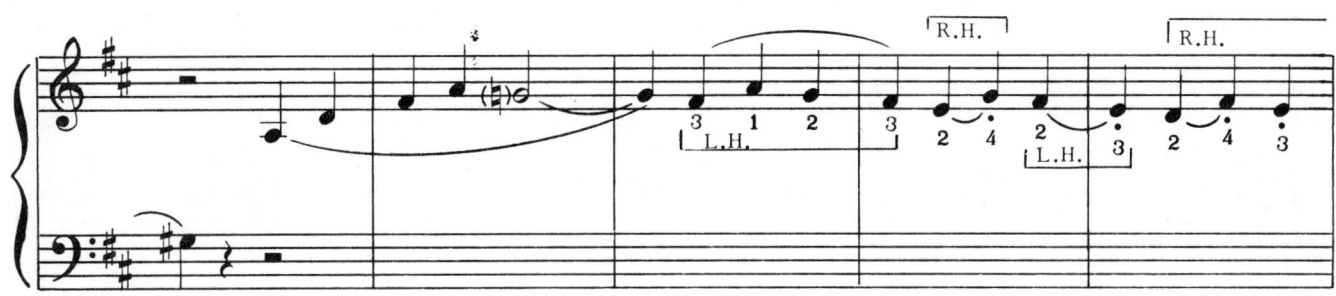

The Wolf

Sneaky (♩ = 84)

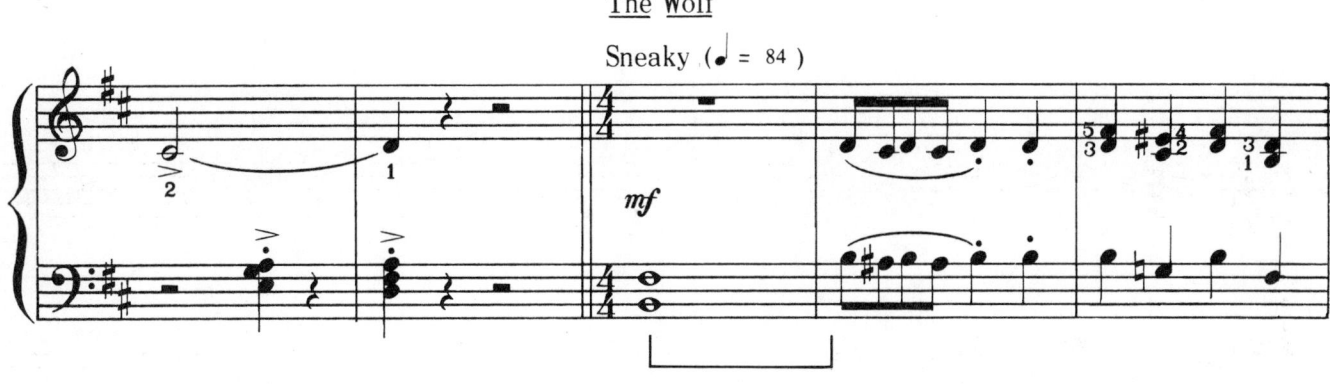

Peter and the Wolf (continued)

The Hunter
March—like (♩ = 108)

Greensleeves

Moderato

ENGLISH (before 1642)
Arr. by RH

Greensleeves (continued)

Variation I

Greensleeves (continued)

Ensembles

Scherzino

MORITZ MOSZKOWSKY (1854–1925)
Arr. by AHZ

Scherzino (continued)

Cradle Song

ROBERT SCHUMANN (1810–1856)
Arr. by AHZ

211

Cradle Song (continued)

March

CORNELIUS GURLITT (1820-1901)
Arr. by AHZ

March (continued)

Allegretto

G. M. MONN (1717–1750)
Arr. by AHZ

Allegretto (continued)

Jigg I

17th CENTURY ENGLISH
Arr. by AHZ

Jigg I (continued)

Jigg II

17th CENTURY ENGLISH
Arr. by AHZ

Jigg II (continued)

Der kleine Wanderer

CORNELIUS GURLITT (1820–1901)
Arr. by AHZ

Der kleine Wanderer (continued)

222

Der kleine Wanderer (continued)

The Reaper

ROBERT SCHUMANN (1810–1856)
Arr. by AHZ

224

The Reaper (continued)

The Reaper (continued)

Appendix

Suggested Goals : First Set

Basic Piano Record of Weekly Performance

Name _____

	Pass	Fail

Goal 1 Major cadence, I IV I$^6_4$ V^7 I, keys through four sharps and four flats, written and played with damper pedal.

Goal 2 Sight read grade I material with both hands.

Goal 3 Folk song harmonization, major, No. 1 and 2.

Goal 4 America, key of G, written and played from memory, pedal added.

Goal 5 Play a duet from Section Five.

Goal 6 Folk song harmonization, major, No. 3 and 4.

Goal 7 Transpose "Hot Cross Buns" up and down a major second and third.

Goal 8 Sight read grade I material with both hands.

Goal 9 Play a duet from Section Seven.

Goal 10 Transpose "Winter's Past", p. 91 up and down minor second and third.

Goal 11 Folk song harmonization No. 5 and review.

Goal 12 Sight read easy (grade 1-2) hymn material, both hands.

Goal 13 America, key of F, written and played, by memory, with pedal.

Goal 14 A solo, well prepared.

Goal 15 Review any goals not yet passed.

Thirty minutes of daily practice is the minimum needed to meet these requirements.
All goals must be passed when due.

Suggested Goals : Second Set

Basic Piano Record of Weekly Performance

Name _____

	Pass	Fail
Goal 1 Minor cadence, I IV I⁶₄ V⁷ I, keys through four sharps and four flats, written and played with damper pedal.		
Goal 2 America the Beautiful written and played by memory with damper pedal.		
Goal 3 Sight read grade 2 material with both hands.		
Goal 4 Folk song harmonization, minor, No. 1 and 2.		
Goal 5 Play a duet from Section Five or Seven.		
Goal 6 Folk Song harmonization, minor key.		
Goal 7 Transpose "Poor Man, Poor Man" up and down a major second and third.		
Goal 8 Sight read grade 2 material with both hands.		
Goal 9 Play a duet from Section Seven.		
Goal 10 Sight read a four part hymn.		
Goal 11 Folk Song Harmonization No. 5.		
Goal 12 Transpose a hymn.		
Goal 13 Play a community song.		
Goal 14 Play a solo.		
Goal 15 Review any goals not yet passed.		

Thirty minutes of daily practice is the minimum to meet these requirements.
All goals must be passed when due.